HOW TO DESIGN & BUILD
FENCES & GATES

*Created and designed
by the editorial staff
of ORTHO Books*

Writer
Diane Snow

Designers
Neil Shakery
Sandy McHenry

Illustrators
Mark Pechenik
Pamela Manley
Patrick Swann
Kathryn Williamson

Major Photography
Laurie Black

Ortho Books

Publisher
Robert L. Iacopi

Editorial Director
Min S. Yee

Managing Editors
Anne Coolman
Michael D. Smith
Sally W. Smith

Production Manager
Ernie S. Tasaki

Editors
Jim Beley
Susan Lammers
Deni Stein

System Manager
Christopher Banks

System Consultant
Mark Zielinski

Asst. System Managers
Linda Bouchard
William F. Yusavage

Photographic Director
Alan Copeland

Photographers
Laurie A. Black
Richard A. Christman

Asst. Production Manager
Darcie S. Furlan

Associate Editors
Richard H. Bond
Alice E. Mace

Production Editors
Don Mosley
Kate O'Keeffe

Chief Copy Editor
Rebecca Pepper

Photo Editors
Anne Pederson
Pam Peirce

National Sales Manager
Garry P. Wellman

Sales Associate
Susan B. Boyle

Operations Director
William T. Pletcher

Operations Assistant
Gail L. Davis

Administrative Assistant
Georgiann Wright

Address all inquiries to
Ortho Books
Chevron Chemical Company
Consumer Products Division
Box 5047
San Ramon, CA 94583

Acknowledgments

"Mending Wall"
From THE POETRY OF ROBERT FROST
Edited by Edward Connery Lathem. Copyright
1930, 1939, © 1969 by Holt, Rinehart and
Winston. Copyright © 1958 by Robert Frost.
Copyright © 1967 by Lesley Frost Ballantine.
Reprinted by permission of Holt, Rinehart and
Winston, Publishers.

Additional Photographers
Carol Bernson: pp. 4–5, 82 (top)
The Colonial Williamsburg Foundation: p. 1
Barbara Engh/California Redwood Association:
    pp. 6–7
Susan Lammers: pp. 8–9
Michael Landis: back cover (lower left), pp. 78–79
Michael McKinley: p. 80
Ortho Photo Library: p. 25 (top)

Fence Designers
Pages 6–7: Ralph W. Jones, Oakland, CA
Pages 10–11: Warren & Chula Camp,
    San Francisco, CA
Pages 16–17, 24, and 82 (bottom): Helen Craddick,
    Cole-Wheatman Designers, San Francisco, CA
Page 81 (bottom): George W. Girvin, Royston,
    Hanamoto, Alley & Abey, Mill Valley, CA

Manuscript Consultants
Robert J. Beckstrom
Berkeley, CA

Pete Wilkinson
Walnut Creek, CA

T. Jeff Williams
Potter Valley, CA

Special Thanks to:
Susan Q. Bruno
Victor Dove
Charlene Draheim
Elvia Fernadez Garwood
Gary W. Lewis
Mike Michael
Bill Mierky
V. C. Morrissey
Diane Parker
Michael & Suzanne Pickett
Mr. & Mrs. Robert Quinlin
Mr. and Mrs. John Paine Renshaw
Mr. & Mrs. Van Muer
Mr. & Mrs. Elwood W. Veliquette
Charlie Walker
Ann Walther
Nancy Wilson

Technical Consultants
See page 94

Front Cover:

Scalloped pickets are a delightful way to create a
boundary, marking a private but open space for all to
enjoy.

Page 1:

Generations ago, someone had a bright design
idea—to bound a pretty little parterre with a
protective line of pickets. The time: the 1600s.
The place: Williamsburg, Virginia. The purpose: to
meet a legal requirement that all dwelling areas
be fenced—but to please the eye as well!

Back Cover:

Upper left. A latticed arbored archway gives a warm
welcome to vistors, and reveals a matching fence that
shapes and defines another area of the yard.

Upper right. A gate so integral to the fence that when
it's closed, only the hardware reveals its existence.

Lower left. No matter what its style, an open gate is a
gateway, an invitation to another world. Perhaps that's
why gates are so special.

Lower right. White picket tops and post caps soften
the austerity of a formal brick house, and the fence
creates a quiet eddy from the street activity and noise.

Chevron Chemical Company
6001 Bollinger Canyon Road, San Ramon, CA 94583

HOW TO DESIGN & BUILD
FENCES & GATES

Fences 7

Why a Fence? 8
Where to Put the Fence? 20
What Kind of Fence? 24
Making a Building Plan 42
Getting Ready to Build 56
Building the Fence 62

Gates 79

What Kind of Gate? 80
Designing the Gate 84
Gate Hardware 90
Building the Gate 92

Index 95

Metric Chart 96

Something there is that doesn't love a wall,
That sends the frozen-ground-swell under it,
And spills the upper boulders in the sun;
And makes gaps even two can pass abreast.
The work of hunters is another thing:
I have come after them and made repair
Where they have left not one stone on a stone,
But they would have the rabbit out of hiding,
To please the yelping dogs. The gaps I mean,
No one has seen them made or heard them made,
But at spring mending-time we find them there.
I let my neighbor know beyond the hill;
And on a day we meet to walk the line
And set the wall between us once again.
We keep the wall between us as we go.
To each the boulders that have fallen to each.
And some are loaves and so nearly balls
We have to use a spell to make them balance:
"Stay where you are until our backs are turned!"
We wear our fingers rough with handling them.
Oh, just another kind of outdoor game,
One on a side. It comes to little more:
There where it is we do not need the wall:
He is all pine and I am apple orchard.
My apple trees will never get across
And eat the cones under his pines, I tell him
He only says, "Good fences make good neighbors,"
Spring is the mischief in me, and I wonder
If I could put a notion in his head:
"Why do they make good neighbors? Isn't it
Where there are cows? But here there are no cows.
Before I built a wall I'd ask to know
What I was walling in or walling out,
And to whom I was like to give offense.
Something there is that doesn't love a wall,
That wants it down." I could say "Elves" to him,
But it's not elves exactly, and I'd rather
He said it for himself. I see him there
Bringing a stone grasped firmly by the top
In each hand, like an old-stone savage armed.
He moves in darkness as it seems to me,
Not of woods only and the shade of trees
He will not go behind his father's saying,
And he likes having thought of it so well
He says again, "Good fences make good neighbors."

"Mending Wall"
From the poetry of Robert Frost.

FENCES

Whatever thing it is that doesn't love a wall, a part of human nature—some fundamental need—exists that does. That need is for boundaries—to mark, to seclude, to surround, to protect. Fences, by creating a boundary (be it a strong physical boundary or a gentler visual one), meet those needs. They mark limits—an edge where one world ends and another begins—secluding what remains within so that it stays safe, secure, nurtured, and refreshed.

Fences also communicate a functional message. They organize the environment, shape space in a more clearly defined way, and form or guide a pattern of use that supports your ideas of what home life can and should be. Thus, the boundaries you create can be as much a service to you and your household as they are to others who use the site or who simply enjoy passing by.

Though a fence is a simple structure, it has a lot of visual impact, which means that it can play a significant part in the impression your property creates and in the feeling it gives. When a fence is thoughtfully planned, carefully designed, and well crafted, that impression can be strikingly beautiful no matter how simple or complex a style it is. Your home and property afford more comfort and become a more pleasant place to live. And the expenditure of energy, time, and money yield a tremendous return for the effort. When you're through building your fence, perhaps you'll discover that good fences really do make good neighbors after all.

Fences can form a bridge between two worlds—the environment that nature creates and the one man builds. This fence borrows the beauty of both and gracefully joins them together into a handsome boundary—to mark, to seclude, to surround, to protect.

WHY A FENCE?

The idea of building a fence joins you to a long history, a tradition that extends from the depths of the wilderness to the breadth of the plains; and from the farm's back forty to the half-acre suburban homesite or to the tiniest garden on a city lot.

And every fence that was ever built, no matter what its style, had a purpose—a job to do . . . perhaps several jobs at the same time. The circumstances which prompted fence building in other times and other places may have differed from those we specifically face today, but at the heart of all these circumstances, some basic human needs continue to motivate us to build fences.

In order to build the right fence—one that serves your purpose—it's important to clarify what your needs are. For the moment, put the issue of style aside. The first questions to ask yourself are functional ones: What is the purpose of the fence? What problems do you want it to solve? What are the needs of your household? How can the new fence improve the site? In short, what are your practical goals? Do you want it to:

• Create a feeling of privacy? Or highlight a nice view or screen an unattractive one?

• Define a special area?

• Provide security and protection for people, pets, and property?

• Buffer the effects of climate or noise?

• Enhance the appearance of your property?

These questions characterize the basic reasons why people build fences. Which are the ones that motivate you most strongly? Rank them in order of their importance to you, in order of their ability to improve your

situation. You'll find that some of them have top priority, others are less essential, and some have no importance to you whatsoever.

The photographs on these and the next two pages show examples of fences in action. They illustrate the principles of function at work. You'll see that, depending on its design, a fence can serve several purposes at the same time. As you look at the photographs, list your own priorities and keep them in mind as you decide the location and style of your fence.

Marking a boundary.
Fences can serve the simple purpose of marking a boundary—the entire perimeter of your property, for example, or just one special area within it. Whether or not this is its main purpose, every fence marks a boundary, both visually and physically. It divides and separates, punctuating the difference between "this" and "that," separating public property from your private world, for instance, or a vegetable garden from a short-cropped lawn. A boundary fence organizes the landscape by giving it visual definition. Fences that mark boundaries also establish perceptual guidelines and patterns of use by clearly defining limits. If, for example, shortcutters have fashioned an unintended path across your lawn, a boundary fence can change that pattern. In the photo at right, a sidewalk boundary of pickets guides the way to the entry path. Spired post caps reinforce the picket tops, creating a pleasing rhythmic pattern along the border of this property.

WHY A FENCE?

Creating privacy. *Fences that are eye level or taller can give a feeling of visual closure and privacy whether or not they are solid surfaces. Openwork fences—such as latticework, spaced slats, or even a completely open grid of 2 by 4s—can still give a feeling of closure and privacy because the eye tends to stop at the fence, where it is captured by the pattern itself and does not see what lies beyond. When selecting a fence style for privacy, you needn't limit yourself to solid, wall-like fences, particularly if you are enclosing small spaces. This slatted fence proves the point. Property lines intersect at an acute angle—typically, a less than pleasant area to be in. Here, the fence provides a delightful solution by creating a space that becomes at once cozy and unconstrained. The "roof" suggests shelter overhead, and the spaces between the slats expand the dimensions of the space to the natural woods beyond.*

WHY A FENCE?

Shaping and defining space. A section of fence can shape a large, undefined area into smaller ones, creating special places with special purposes. You can transform a nondescript front walk into a more refined and formal entry or into a receptive and welcoming one. You can create a garden work or storage area or a protected garbage-can enclosure. Or you can introduce a pleasant feeling of background or enclosure in an open and diffuse space such as a large patio or terrace. When thinking about fences, include the possibility of strategically placed fence sections. In the lattice grid fence shown here, large-scaled openings work to screen one area from another without impeding the feeling of essential connection between them. The visual separation creates a special place that is certainly part of a larger whole, but nonetheless merits distinction.

WHY A FENCE?

Providing protection and security. *Unless you want them to, fences needn't look like barricades in order to protect and secure. Even low fences, or open, lightweight ones, can be effective for security fencing simply because they suggest limits and invite people to respect those limits. They deter unwanted entrants psychologically rather than physically. The strength of the infill and the height of the fence affect the amount of security and protection you can achieve. Gauge how much actual protection you need. Choose a style of fence that will give you what you need without imprisoning you. Though the message of the fence shown here isn't strident, it's made quite clear: entry is gained by the occupants' permission. Even when strict security measures are required, such as an electronic admission system, the fence treatment can be gracious. When you choose a fence style and finish that blend with the existing architecture, your functional needs are served but are attractively discreet.*

WHY A FENCE?

Buffering the effects of climate and noise. *Fences can soften the harsh effects of chilling winds, beating rain, glaring sun, and drifting snow. Generally, infill with very small or medium-sized openings works best, no matter what type of material the fence is made of. This type of infill breaks, filters, or scatters the environmental forces into softer, more diffuse forms. A fence can't actually exclude noise the way a thick wall can unless it is high enough to block sound waves and is sheathed with solid infill on both sides. On the other hand, a fence can do a lot to insulate you from the annoyance of noise by buffering your perception of it. If you can't readily see the source of noise, your awareness of it is minimized. The higher the fence, and the less you can see directly through it, the more effective the barrier you create. When house and yard are situated close to the street, such as the one in this photograph, a fence helps buffer the effects of noise, no matter how much traffic or activity the street might carry. What takes place on the outside of the fence remains unseen, so that the ambience created on the inside of the fence line is one you'd like to live with and enjoy.*

WHY A FENCE?

Enhancing the look of the house. *Sometimes the sole purpose of a fence is to improve the overall look of the house and property. Because fences form a vertical plane, you can use this plane itself—style, finish, and trim details aside—to reconfigure space and improve the overall ambience of your property. If, for example, your home is like a tiny island floating in an unbounded sea of landscaping, you can flank it with fencing. Planes of fence on either side of a house extend it, giving the impression that it spans the width of the lot and is anchored in its space. Or, if the house is so close to the street that it seems to be in constant contact with the rush and tumble of public life, even a low fence can baffle the onslaught and create a little pocket of calm behind it. The fence shown here illustrates this principle and achieves its aim in appropriate style. White pointed pickets reinforce the existing architectural theme and gives an open, friendly feeling. Yet, it also diffuses street-side activity so that worldly cares can be set aside before stepping inside the door.*

WHERE TO PUT THE FENCE?

Your priorities and the site itself work together to help you decide where to locate the fence line. The site has a set of "givens"—some are features you like and want to retain; others are features you might wish to improve if you had the chance. A new fence gives you that chance.

By discovering for yourself what the "givens" are (see the illustration on the facing page), and by planning the new fence line carefully, you'll find that your fence can transform your site in many pleasing ways. There are two approaches to planning your fence line. They are equally effective, so choose the one that is easier for you.

One is to plan it out on paper, using a site plan of your property as a base drawing and tracing-paper overlays to try out alternative fence-line schemes. Planning with pencil and paper is the fastest, easiest way to arrive at a pleasing solution, but you need a site plan to do this. You can draw one in an hour or two, or you can try to find a copy of your site plan. If yours is a newer home or one that was specially designed, or if your property has had professional landscape work done, contact the appropriate sources—the building department, the designer or architect, the building contractor, the landscape contractor, or even the previous owner—to see if you can locate one.

The other approach is to plan your fence line right on the property itself; mark the line with stakes and string, and reposition them until the fence line is suitably located. When you have a helper, you'll be more likely to experiment with alternative layouts and work out the fine points.

How to Draw a Site Plan

1. Make a sketch of your lot on a piece of paper. Include the property lines, the house, driveway, patios, walkways, garden beds, and any other features that you want to see on the completed site plan.

2. Take field measurements. Use a helper to hold the other end of a 50- or 100-foot tape. Measure the perimeter of the site, recording the dimensions on your sketch as you go. Measure whatever features you have included on your sketch.

3. Transfer field measurements to ¼-inch-scale graph paper. Plot out the property lines. Locate and sketch in all the other site features you measured out. Work lightly in pencil. When everything is in place and the site is visually represented, go back and darken the lines.

If you note dimensions and the distances between things, on your site plan as you draw it, you will save yourself the time of counting out squares to calculate distances later. Keep in mind that this drawing need not look like an architect did it; if it is accurate and legible to you, it will serve your purposes just fine.

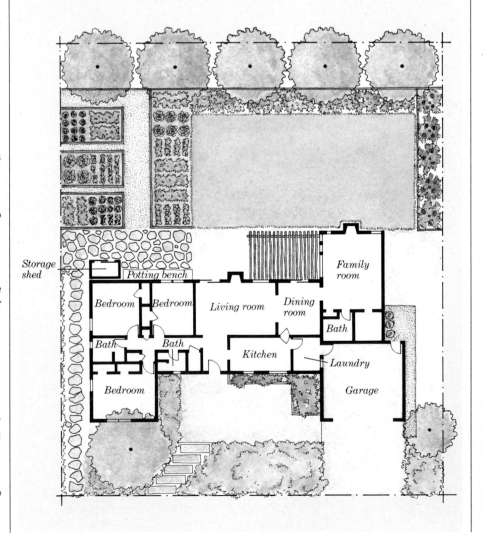

Establish Your Layout Priorities

Use your priorities to suggest a rough outline for the fence line. Where is it needed to do the job you want it to do? Read your list of priorities and ask yourself *where?* for each one. Then jot down your answer. If you keep in mind who the fence is for—your pet, your child, your neighbor—you will have a good starting point.

Next, take a look at your home and property from three perspectives: from inside the house, from the outdoors, and from the neighborhood beyond your property lines. As you do so, ask yourself the following questions:

1. What are the "givens"—those features you like and want to retain, and those you don't like and want to improve or camouflage?

2. Where are the activity areas? What are they used for?

3. What are the traffic patterns—from the street to the house, from the house to the outside areas, and from one area to another?

4. How wide should openings in the fence be to accommodate these traffic paths?

5. What surrounding views would you like to retain?

6. Which views into your property would you like to block?

7. What areas on the site would you like to mask or conceal, and from what vantage point?

8. What is the direction of prevailing winds that you'd like to block or soften?

9. What is the source of noise you'd like to exclude?

10. Where does the sun rise and set in relation to your property?

A good way to get an overview of these issues is to map them out on a site plan. On a tissue overlay, draw circles for activity areas, arrows for traffic paths, wavy lines for winds, and so on. Such a map of your property helps you see how these issues affect the placement of your fence. After studying this map, you can plot your fence line with full confidence that it will accomplish your goals.

How Your Site Works

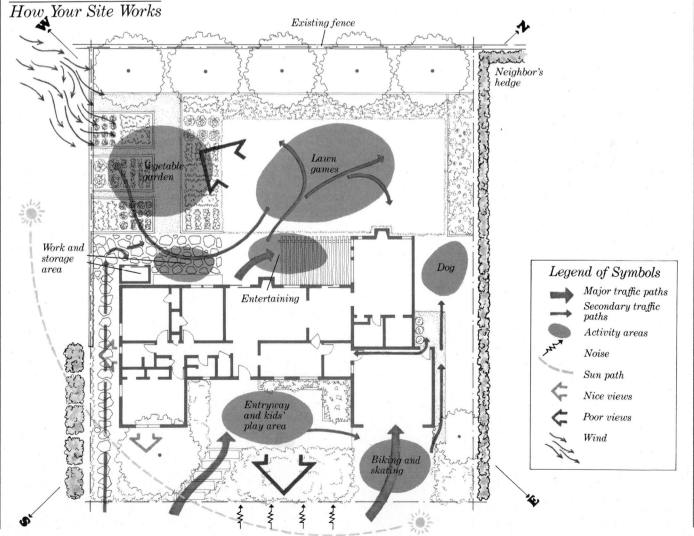

Existing fence

Neighbor's hedge

Vegetable garden

Lawn games

Work and storage area

Entertaining

Dog

Entryway and kids' play area

Biking and skating

Legend of Symbols

Major traffic paths

Secondary traffic paths

Activity areas

Noise

Sun path

Nice views

Poor views

Wind

WHERE TO PUT THE FENCE?

Make a Rough Layout

When you have a clear sense of the issues you want to deal with, try out some of them on paper or in the field to see how they feel. Don't labor over any one layout scheme; in fact, you'll have more fun and find the best solution if you work freely and quickly. Dream a little. Use the book for ideas, or try some fanciful notion from your own imagination; this is how to get one idea to lead to another and on to the actual plan. On the facing page, you'll see the basic rules of thumb on gates. For a fuller view of gate design considerations, see pages 79-93. Make a layout, stand back and look at it, and make any improvements that are needed. There are no hard and fast rules for shaping a good fence line, but there are two ideals to aim for:

- Keep it simple.
- Be generous in shaping outdoor space.

A simple straight fence, well designed and well built, has enough beauty in its own right to hold the eye with interest. Fancy jogs in the fence line are distracting (and extra work) unless they serve a purpose.

By its own nature, outdoor space is expansive. Tight, stingy spaces make people feel boxed in, which is at odds with the natural feeling of the environment. Even service areas should be large enough so you can move comfortably around in them. And certainly, areas for outdoor living should feel ample and free.

Sketch the Layout

When your ideas have jelled and you've got the fence line where you want it, with gate openings sized and placed, make a sketch of the plan. If you were laying it out in the field, measure the distance of each length of fence and the width of each opening, and record the dimensions on a sketch. If you were planning on pa-

per from the start, make a sketch of the final plan on a fresh tracing-paper overlay and record the dimensions of the planned fence line.

This plan will be used to help you figure out the spacing between posts when you divide the line into bays (pages 54-55), when you compute the materials you'll need, and when you actually stake the layout before beginning construction.

Legal Considerations

Two important legal considerations go hand in hand with fence building: building codes and property lines.

Building codes. Many communities have established building codes that define basic design and construction requirements for fencing. Their purpose is to ensure that individual actions don't infringe on the rights of others—rights to bodily safety, fresh air, sunlight, views, and other environmental factors that might affect the public good.

To find out what, if any, requirements or restrictions will pertain to your new fence, call the local building inspector, who will provide appropriate guidelines. If there are good reasons to relax the requirements in favor of your plans, the building department can tell you how to get a variance. The aim of the department is to be of service, and the advice, help, and guidance given are free.

Property lines. It is important that you know the location of your property lines; if any part of the new fence should encroach on your neighbor's property, you will be the one responsible for moving it in case your neighbor objects. Unless you and your neighbor jointly own and share responsibility for the fence (outlined in writing), the new fence installation must be wholly within the bounds of your own property, concrete footings included.

Finding the property lines, the legal boundaries, can be tricky. Boundary markers might be as transient as a wooden stake, which rots out; or a stone or metal pipe, which can be

knocked out of place, covered with earth, or otherwise concealed.

In many instances you will be able to locate the boundaries from a boundary map which might be on file with the lending institution that handles your mortgage, or at your local building department. Alternately, you may be able to locate the boundaries by following the written description of your property lines outlined in your deed. If you can't get a clear idea that way, your neighbors' understanding of where the boundaries are can also help you establish a workable fence line. But be aware that this joint determination is more a ''gentleman's agreement'' than actual boundary facts; so it is best to get the shared understanding in writing for everyone's sake—including that of future owners.

If it is difficult to reach an understanding of the boundaries, and you'd like to ensure that no future disputes arise, you might opt to have your site resurveyed (for a fee) by a surveyor or civil engineer.

Draw the Final Fence Line

To draw the final fence line plan, do the following:

1. Tape a piece of tracing paper to the site plan. Make a little circle where the boundary lines intersect (this makes it easy to get the overlay located again if you want to remove it and reposition it later).

2. Trace out the fence layout you have in mind. Leave a break in the fence line to show where openings will be. If you plan to put a gate there, indicate the direction of the swing.

3. If in the course of making this sketch of your first idea you find there are things about the layout that you want to improve and change, jot down a few notes on the side of the tracing paper to remind you. Make as many sketches as you need.

Guidelines for Planning Gate Openings

In addition to the gate design and construction considerations discussed on pages 79-89, there are some functional issues you'll want to consider as you plan the width of gate openings.

For foot traffic, an opening 3 feet wide is just big enough for a person and a large piece of equipment to pass comfortably through. A 4-foot-wide opening is just enough for two people to walk through together, and a 6-foot-wide opening is ample enough to accommodate a group of several people.

For vehicular traffic, make the opening about 10 feet wide (or less if you're careful when driving through). The best way to get a sense of how wide the opening should be is to measure out a couple of options and see how comfortable the access feels.

Plotting the Fence Line

The household on this piece of property has priorities that stack up like this: The new fence should 1) Provide Protection (Where? In the back yard—to keep neighborhood dogs out, the kids and your dog in. On the front patio—for the kids.) 2) Create Privacy (Where? On the front patio.) 3) Shape and Define Space (Where? Around the back patio and lawn.) 4) Enhance the Site (Where? Along the front of the property.) 5) Block Noise (Where? Around the front patio.) 6) Conceal Unsightly Areas (Where? Near the garbage cans by the work yard and vegetable garden.)

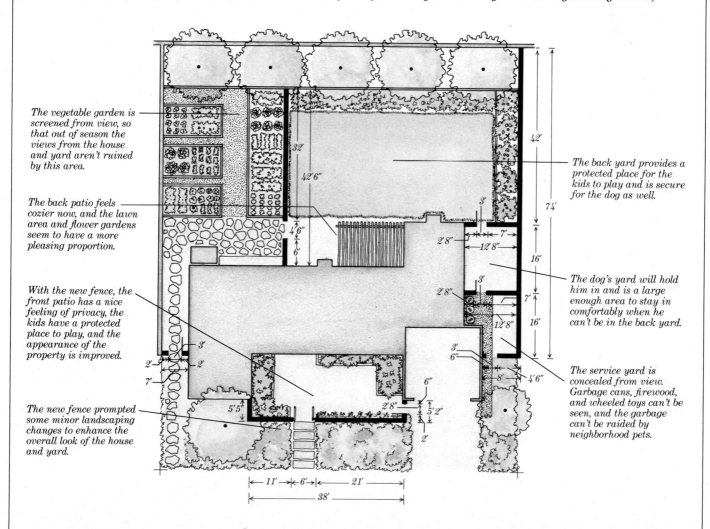

The vegetable garden is screened from view, so that out of season the views from the house and yard aren't ruined by this area.

The back patio feels cozier now, and the lawn area and flower gardens seem to have a more pleasing proportion.

With the new fence, the front patio has a nice feeling of privacy, the kids have a protected place to play, and the appearance of the property is improved.

The new fence prompted some minor landscaping changes to enhance the overall look of the house and yard.

The back yard provides a protected place for the kids to play and is secure for the dog as well.

The dog's yard will hold him in and is a large enough area to stay in comfortably when he can't be in the back yard.

The service yard is concealed from view. Garbage cans, firewood, and wheeled toys can't be seen, and the garbage can't be raided by neighborhood pets.

WHAT KIND OF FENCE?

Given your functional priorities, the issue of fence style begins to take on new meaning. The style you choose must serve two purposes: It should be visually appealing, but it must also meet your functional needs.

On the pages that follow, you will find a compendium of classic fence styles using a range of common materials. These illustrated descriptions will help you compare different fence materials and styles with regard to your own needs. As you look at these illustrations, keep your functional goals in mind. In addition, think about aesthetics from the broadest perspective: Consider how you want your new fence to relate to your existing site. Your home and property already express a certain design theme, a particular character. The features that make up this character are the architectural style of the dwelling and the nature of the landscaping. The fence, as the newcomer in this setting, will work best if it harmonizes with the established design themes.

Fences create a strong visual impression. In one setting, a certain type of fencing material in a particular style and finish can be a stunning complement to the property. In a different setting, the same fence might seem awkward and uncomfortably out of place.

Before selecting a specific style, see which of the basic site-design approaches (characterized in the photographs here) will give you the quality of feeling you'd like your new fence to bring to the site. Then use the illustrations on the pages that follow to help you answer the question, What kind of fence?

How will your new fence relate to the character of your site? Will it join forces with the architectural style of the house and remain prominent, separate, and distinct from the garden it surrounds? This fence extends the proportions of the house and creates an open-air room by shaping a half-wall enclosure.

Above: *Will it join forces with the yard and garden, blending with the out-of-doors, becoming a subtle complement to landscaping and plantings? Roses ramble in rapt delight along this modest rail fence, creating a quiet and beautiful blend.*

Right: *Will it form a link between the natural environment (the garden) and the built environment (the architecture) by borrowing design themes and finish treatments from both? Lining the property edge with architectural order which matches the style of the house, these white pickets also invite the meandering growth of living things.*

Fence Styles

On the next 16 pages you'll see for yourself how versatile fence styles can be. This is due to differences inherent in the building materials themselves (wood looks very different from glass; bamboo looks very different from metal) and to variations in the way those materials are assembled to form the fence.

In the illustrations, the frame for each fence remains essentially the same except for changes in height. This helps you see both the aesthetic and functional characteristics of a fence without confusing the issue by including structural characteristics as well. (Structural variations can also make a big difference in the design of a fence. See pages 44-49.)

The chart accompanying each illustration tells you how well each type of fence provides protection, creates privacy, and so on. The text discusses the nature of the infill—its ambient qualities and the feeling it projects to focus your selection from an aesthetic and a practical point of view.

Once you've chosen a basic style that appeals to you, you can use each illustration in another way. The construction details included are the actual specifications for that fence. The dimensions of one bay and each of its component parts are all you need to know to build that fence to any length, for any layout you plan. If you decide to use one of these designs exactly as shown, pages 20-23 show you how to decide where to put the fence. Next, pages 50-51 help you negotiate slopes and obstructions, and pages 56-61 get you ready to build. Then, on page 62, instructions for building the fence begin.

You also have another option: Use the illustrated fence style as a basis for designing your own custom fence. Small variations in any of its component parts make a big difference in how a fence looks. Experimenting with these variations and creating a special design can be as much fun as enjoying the finished product. To design your own fence, choose a fence style from the next 16 pages, and then continue through the design sequence outlined on pages 44-49, choosing whatever design variations appeal to you. By the time you've finished your custom design, you might surprise yourself with your success! When you've completed your basic design, plan your fence layout and complete the specifications for building (pages 52-55).

Metal Fences

This book focuses on designing and building wood-frame fences. You'll find brief descriptions of chain link and ornamental iron fences on pages 40 and 41, but in general, the design, fabrication, and installation of metal fences are best turned over to professionals or specialists. Metal materials have little tolerance for error, and it takes experience to learn to deal with them skillfully enough to complete a project with a feeling of success. Look in the *Yellow Pages* under Fencing Materials, Ornamental Iron, and Fencing Contractors.

Stacked Rails

The stacked-rail fence (also called a pole fence) is the original American fence. It's still a beautiful style for ambling along a country road. Traditionally, this type of fence was made of trees or saplings that had been stripped of limbs and then stacked in a simple zigzag line. Lumber suppliers specializing in fencing materials carry rails that are split by hand. The rails are typically 8 feet long, of moderate cost, and fence construction time is low.

Protection and security. Moderate. It can keep people and pets in or out, but is easy to climb over.

Visual privacy. None.

Tempering the environment. Will block drifting snow but little else.

Defining space. The bold and broad outline creates an interesting perimeter boundary.

Suitable finish treatment. Let it weather naturally.

Double Posts and Rails

The double-post-and-rail fence is the child of the zigzag stacked-rail fence, but is straightened out and held upright with two confining posts on each side of the stack. It has the same rustic, rugged, and enduring look and much of the beauty of the zigzag style, but it takes up less space and costs less because it covers less distance. Construction time is low.

Protection and security. Moderate. It can keep people and pets in or out, but is easy to climb over.

Visual privacy. None.

Tempering the environment. Will block drifting snow but little else.

Defining space. Good. It clearly delineates a boundary. It is best seen at a distance.

Suitable finish treatment. Let it weather naturally.

Wire

8' split-rail

36"

Posts and Boards

Post-and-board fences came into common use when machines and mobility allowed sawyers to take their milling equipment from farm to farm. Logs could now be sawed into boards and other construction materials at the farm site. They are simple, modest, and quite beautiful in open, country settings. Boards are sold by the linear foot, according to the thickness and width of the piece. Both cost and building time are low.

Protection and security. Moderate. Provides the feeling of protection, but is easy to climb over.

Visual privacy. Very little.

Tempering the environment. Will block drifting snow but little else.

Defining space. Good. Attractively marks a simple boundary.

Suitable finish treatment. Stain, paint, or let it weather naturally.

2x8

1x8

1½"

1x4

1x8

36"

Boards

Board fences are the most uncommonly common type of fence you can build: common because there are so many types of them, uncommon because even small variations in the configuration of parts change the appearance remarkably. All the variations illustrated below and on the next two pages are common board fences, demonstrating just how uncommon they can be.

Boards can be purchased in standard sizes and shapes at building supply outlets. The cost varies from moderate to high, depending on the lumber and the style you build. Construction time depends on the style of fence; it generally ranges from moderate to high.

Protection and security. Depending on the height, and on how close together the boards are placed, it can provide a high level of both.

Visual privacy. Closed styles can provide total closure. Semiopen styles provide somewhat less.

Tempering the environment. The closed surface blocks noise and sun but forces wind into downdrafts.

Defining space. If boards are closely spaced, can literally define space the way a wall does. Can seem heavy-handed unless softened by plantings.

Suitable finish treatment. Stain, paint, or let it weather naturally.

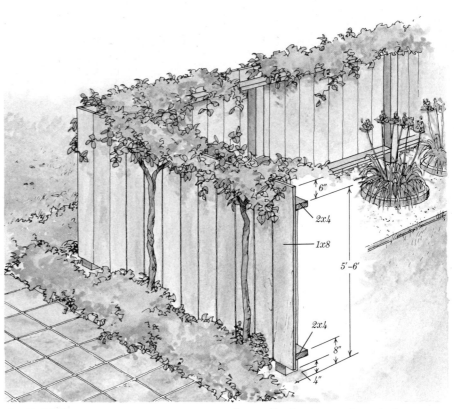

Variations

The basic board fence (seen above) has a kaleidoscopic capacity. Surprisingly tiny changes in its basic design can produce big differences in the appearance of each fence. The examples on these pages demonstrate this principle. Building materials remain basically the same, though the way in which they are assembled produces distinctly different styles. The changes are: board placements (edges can abut, overlap, or have spaces between); board size (they can be mixed in repeating patterns); and orientation (boards can run diagonally or horizontally).

Boards and slats, with spaces between them, compose a fence with a light look and a pleasing visual rhythm. The surface is semiclosed, which yields ample privacy and an everchanging play of light and shadow. The widths of the boards, and the amount of space left between them, is a matter of creative choice. It is a quick, easy style to build; it requires a little less material than the basic board fence; and it offers high aesthetic returns in its simplicity, refinement, and appealing proportions.

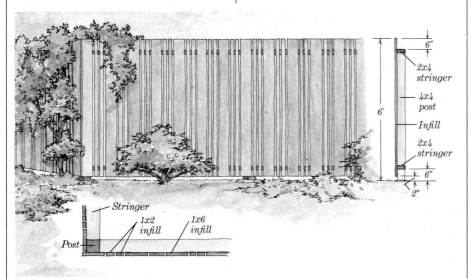

Featherboard fences are classic, condensed versions of the louver style. Boards are mounted between a paired set of horizontal nailers with each board edge overlapping the next. This produces a fully closed fence for maximum privacy, and lends a pleasant pattern of shadow-highlighted textural interest as well. Construction requires a little extra time, since overlapping board edges must be carefully positioned and the infill is inset to the frame. Its cost is about equal to that of the basic board fence.

Board-on-board fences give a fully closed fence surface, and therefore offer full privacy, but that's not all. Because the boards are fastened to one central nailer but change sides board by board, the configuration allows gentle passage of breezes and free ventilation. The infill is inset to the frame, which requires some care in fitting, but it's worth the effort. The look is clean lined, slim, and nicely scaled. The cost is about equal to that of the basic board fence.

Alternating board widths is another way of adding rhythm and scale to a simple, straightforward board fence. The shift from wide to narrow sets a pattern that is distinctive, yet calm. Board edges abut, and at each joint, a subtle shadow line is produced, which delicately punctuates the vertical direction. The cost, installation time, and degree of privacy are equal to those of the basic board fence, but the visual effect is richer.

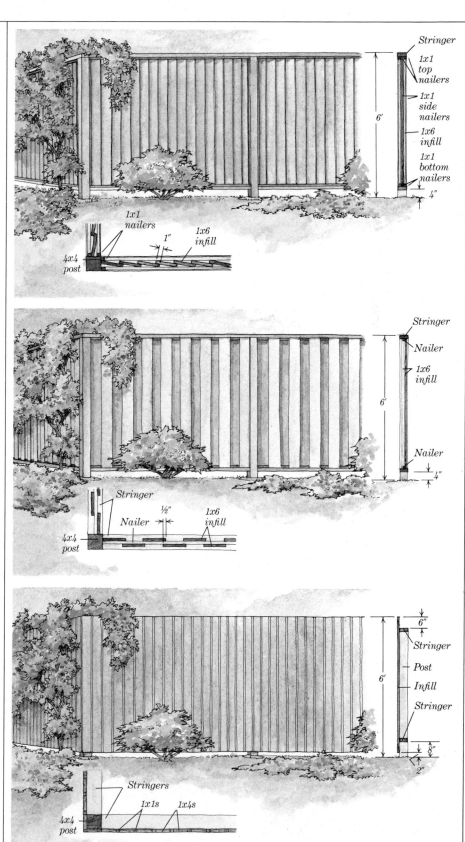

29

Fence Styles

Board-and-batten fences achieve a bold textural effect and create a strong, massive feeling with appealing grace. Boards are mounted on the fence framework first, and then battens are fastened to the boards at each joint. Even if the boards shrink as they season, the battens conceal the gaps, so complete privacy is ensured over time. Both construction time and cost are high, but functionally and aesthetically, it may be a worthwhile investment.

Alternating bays is a nice way to share an attractive fence with your neighbors. Here, the boards are fastened to the frame horizontally and bay-by-bay, and the view changes from a frame exposed to a frame concealed right on down the line. This variation works as easily with vertically or diagonally mounted infill and still, both sides of the fence are the "good side." Cost and construction time are both the same as for a basic board fence.

Lap-joint grid fences are a pretty way to screen an area without blocking the view. This style invites the eye first to rest on the fence and take in the pattern, and then to see beyond to the background. And it works both ways—views out aren't blocked, but they are screened, so the viewer has a choice. You can get a lot of screen for a small amount of material, but construction time is high, since each board intersection requires a pair of notches to create a flush, lapped joint.

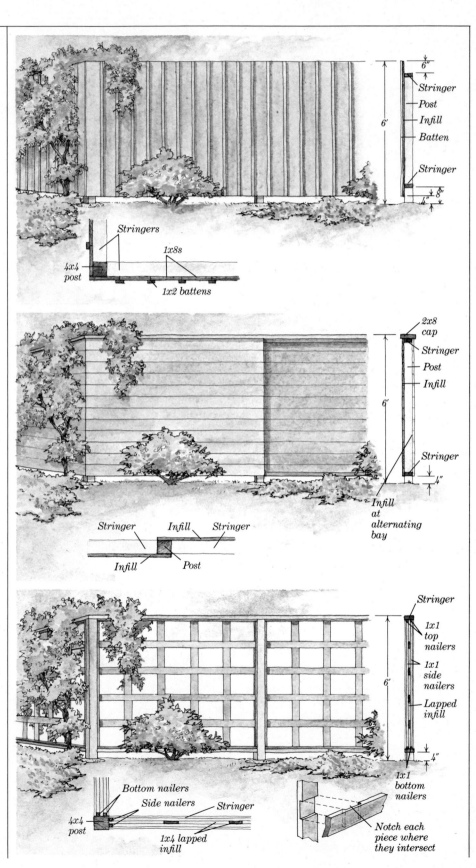

Pickets

Picket fences have an irrepressible charm, and their character has carried them from cottage to village to town to city throughout many generations. They have a welcoming appearance and a gentle way of marking a boundary. Their classic style fits well in many different settings.

The fancy cut tops and special finial frills associated with picket fences in the past are now hard to find. Lumberyards still carry pickets, but only in limited shapes. You can cut your own tops, of course, but that can be quite time-consuming because of the great number of pickets needed to make a fence. Cabinet shops can do special milling and shaping, or the lumberyard may be able to cut the pickets for you for an extra fee. The basic cost for pickets is low, but construction time for a fence is generally medium to high.

Protection and security. Will keep children and pets in or out, and the pointed pickets make the fence tricky to hop over.

Visual privacy. Very little, though pickets tend to capture the eye and hold it.

Tempering the environment. Will block drifting snow, and close spacing between pickets can soften breezes.

Defining space. Good. Clearly defines any boundary.

Suitable finish treatment. Paint generally looks best, but stain can also be effective.

Variations

Pickets offer you a world of variations. Some of the standard ones are shown here, but fancy filigree and other whimsical ways of cutting pickets can delight passersby with their special visual interest. Designing picket tops is a lot of fun, and planning their fabrication is a challenge in ingenuity. Wide-diameter hole saws can easily cut concave curves; a saber or band saw will produce convex ones. To lay out the pickets for shaping, use a hardboard template.

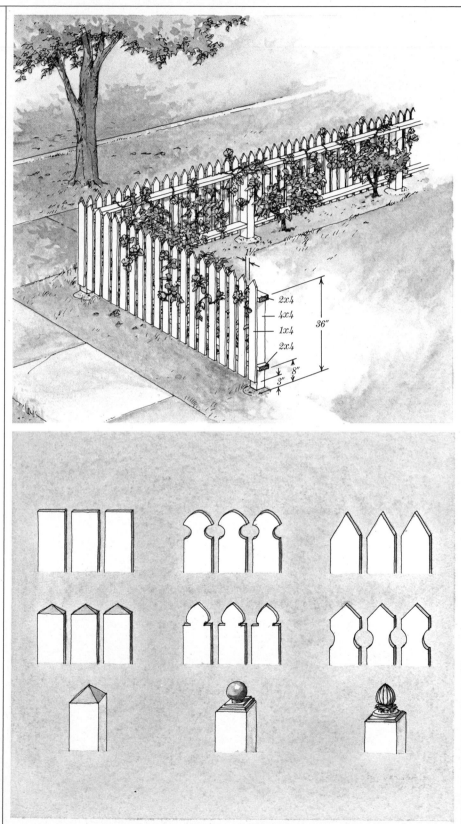

Slats

Slats are similar to pickets but are taller. A slat fence has a simple, crisp look and clean lines. The height of the fence and the relatively small scale of the slats give it a feeling of lightness and refinement.

Slats can be purchased by the piece or by the bundle at lumberyards. Their cost is moderate, though it takes time to assemble a fence of slats. Construction takes a good bit of time.

Protection and security. Can provide a high level of both, depending on how close together the slats are placed. Similar to that of high board fences.

Visual privacy. Good. The fence feels open but is hard to see through.

Tempering the environment. Will block drifting snow and is excellent for softening breezes and filtering light.

Defining space. Good. Defines space with graciousness.

Suitable finish treatment. Paint or let it weather naturally.

Lath

Lath is a standard lumber material that is often used for lattice fences and arbors. It is a very thin material (about ⅜ inch) that is as wide as a slat (1 ½ inch). Its rough surface gives it an informal appearance that is naturally at home in the garden.

Lath is quite inexpensive. It is commonly sold at building supply outlets. All the little pieces, however, take time to nail in place on a fence.

Protection and security. Quite good, though it is stronger if the lath is applied to both sides of the fence.

Visual privacy. Can provide a strong sense of privacy without seeming confining from either side.

Tempering the environment. Very good for filtering sunlight and softening winds.

Defining space. Good. Similar to slats.

Suitable finish treatment. Let it weather naturally.

Stakes

Stakes make a very handsome, sturdy fence with a rich surface texture that easily harmonizes with the landscape and garden. Because they are split, stakes are rough, but they have a look that combines orderly refinement and informality.

Stakes are sold by the piece or by the bundle at lumberyards. Their cost is moderate, and building time is just a bit above average.

Protection and security. Excellent. This is a sturdy, rough-surfaced material.

Visual privacy. Excellent. The infill is solid.

Tempering the environment. Blocks noise and provides shade. It may block wind too abruptly, causing downdrafts.

Defining space. Can be too confining if used around a small area, but very effective when viewed from a distance.

Suitable finish treatment. Stain or let it weather naturally.

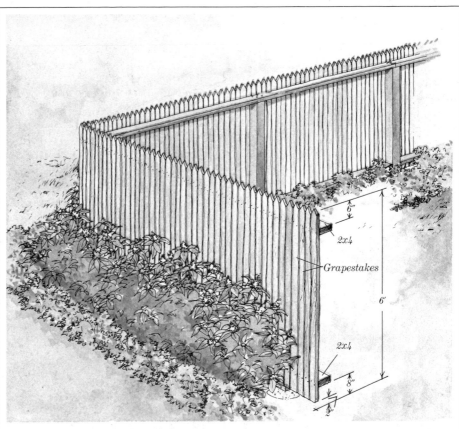

Palings

Palings, sometimes referred to as stockade fencing, are saplings sharpened to a point at the top and split. A paling fence gives the appearance of a dense young forest and works well in a lightly wooded setting. It looks best when left unfinished. Palings may be difficult to find, but lumberyards that specialize in fencing materials may stock them or be able to order them for you. They are expensive, and construction requires a lot of time.

Protection and security. Very good. A paling fence is a scaled-down version of a stockade wall.

Visual privacy. Excellent. Round poles butt tightly for total privacy.

Tempering the environment. Blocks wind, snow, and sun and creates a barrier to noise.

Defining space. Gives such a strong feeling of enclosure that it is best used as perimeter rather than accent fencing.

Suitable finish treatment. Let it weather naturally.

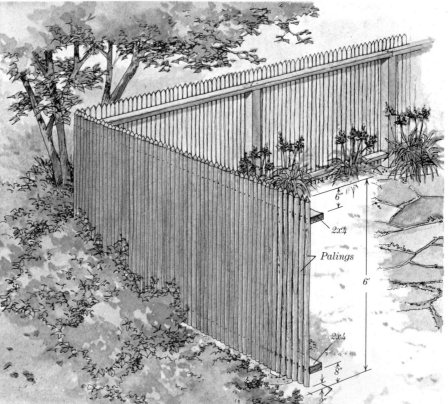

Fence Styles

Lattice

Lattice is a classic in the garden. Persian, Italian, French, and English gardens have used this crisscross style for centuries. Its formal, regular lines become loose and lively with foliage, as light plays across and through it.

Lattice allows you to create a particular rhythm and scale by varying the spacing between members. Prefabricated sheets are available at building suppliers and lumberyards. It's quick and inexpensive to install, and looks best inset to the frame.

Protection and security. Good. Gives both in a pleasant, gentle way.

Visual privacy. Good. Though semiopen, the pattern of the fence holds the eye.

Tempering the environment. Softens wind and filters sunlight.

Defining space. Good. A delightful way to define space and screen an area.

Suitable finish treatment. Paint, stain, or let it weather naturally.

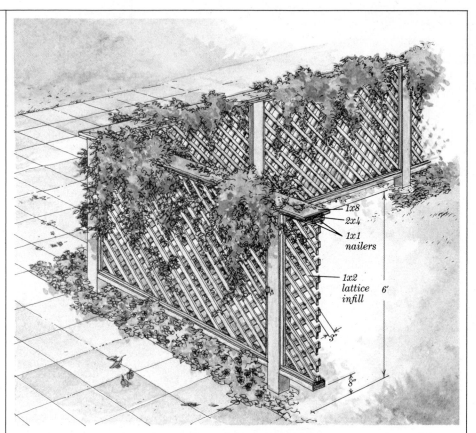

Louvers

Vertical louvers have a clean-lined architectural look, a lot of textural interest, and visual dynamics. Louvers also create interesting patterns of light and shadow.

Since louvers are made of boards, any lumberyard can supply the materials. Because the boards are angled, more are required to cover any span. This makes the louvered fence more expensive than other types of board fencing and more time-consuming to build.

Protection and security. Very good. The fence is sturdy and hard to climb.

Visual privacy. Moderate. Gives closure in one direction and direct line of sight in another.

Tempering the environment. Softens and redirects winds; filters and blocks sunlight.

Defining space. Good for screening, using two or three sections.

Suitable finish treatment. Paint, stain, or let it weather naturally.

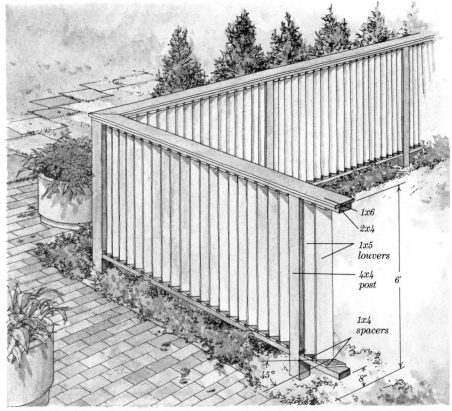

Basket Weave

Basket weave fences are made of boards woven together. They look best if the undulation is minimized, which can be accomplished by using one thin spacer for each bay.

Around a small area, basket weave can be somewhat overwhelming. It is fairly easy to install, though it requires patience and dexterity. Very thin materials look best, are surprisingly strong, and are quite inexpensive. Basket weave materials are sold at lumberyards.

Protection and security. Very good. The weave makes a strong surface.

Visual privacy. Very good. You can't see through it.

Tempering the environment. Good for softening winds and for blocking noise and sun.

Defining space. Can be too dominant for small areas but effective when viewed at a distance.

Suitable finish treatment. Stain or let it weather naturally.

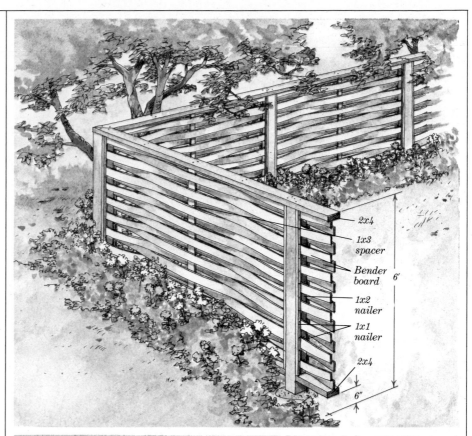

Plywood

A well-proportioned plywood fence can be an extremely elegant, expansive addition, for all its constructional simplicity. Plywood is sold in standard sheet sizes in a range of thicknesses, grades, and surface textures or veneers. Choose materials that are thick enough to resist bowing in heavy wind. Plywood is sold at all lumberyards.

Protection and security. Excellent. Plywood is strong, durable, and difficult to penetrate.

Visual privacy. Excellent. You can't see through it.

Tempering the environment. Blocks sun and noise but can cause strong downdrafts.

Defining space. A very attractive way to define space simply, but it can be overbearing in a small space.

Suitable finish treatment. Paint or stain.

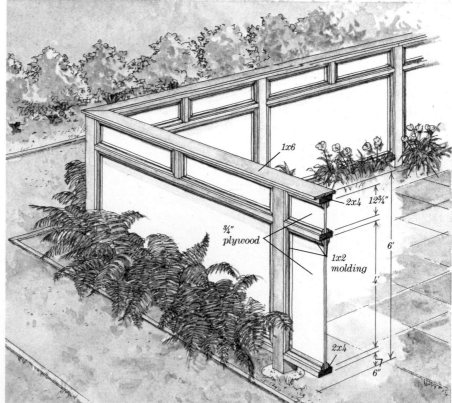

Fence Styles

Clapboard

Under the right conditions, clapboard can be extremely attractive, when it matches your home's siding. Its decidedly horizontal effect provides a wall-like sense of calm and protection. It is best used on level ground or on very gradual, evenly sloping terrain.

Clapboard is sold at building supply outlets. It is not expensive and is fairly easy to put up.

Protection and security. Excellent, especially if the fence is high.

Visual privacy. Excellent. Clapboard creates a solid wall.

Tempering the environment. Blocks noise, sun, and snow; can cause downdrafts.

Defining space. Feels architectural and permanent; might be overbearing in a small space.

Suitable finish treatment. Paint both sides of the fence and cap off the top for the best appearance.

Tongue-and-Groove

Tongue-and-groove materials create a soundly solid infill for fencing, since the edges interlock. The effect is simple, attractive, and orderly. Tiny shadow lines where the boards interlock give a subtle yet perceptible visual rhythm.

This type of lumber is sold at lumberyards and can be expensive. Construction time is moderately high, since the boards are inset to the frame and require some fitting.

Protection and security. Excellent. These materials are strong, and the surface is solid.

Visual privacy. Excellent. The interlocking edges create a solid wall.

Tempering the environment. Blocks sun; thicker materials buffer noise.

Defining space. Good, although solid fencing can be overbearing in a small space.

Suitable finish treatment. Paint, stain, or let it weather naturally.

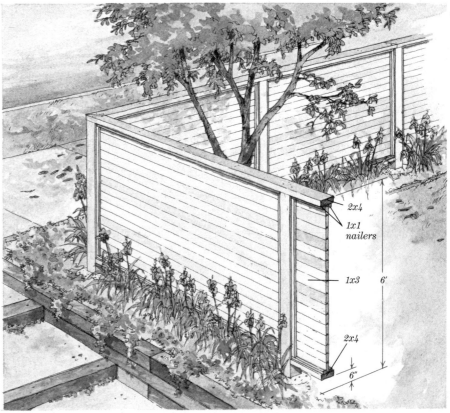

Shingles

Shingles provide a highly textured fence surface, giving an appearance that is rich, warm, and quite wall-like. If your dwelling is shingled also, it can unify the site.

Shingles are sold by the bundle at lumberyards and are not expensive. It takes a lot of time to install shingles, since each has to be nailed individually. Shingles need to be fastened to a backing surface such as an existing fence, plywood, or furring strips.

Protection and security. Excellent, since a shingled fence is much like a wall.

Visual privacy. Excellent. The taller the fence, the better.

Tempering the environment. Blocks sun and noise quite effectively. Can cause downdrafts.

Defining space. Gives a strong feeling of definition and coziness, but can be too confining in a small area.

Suitable finish treatment. Paint, stain, or let it weather naturally.

2x8 cap

2x4

1x2 molding

Shingles

Plywood

36"

3"

2x4

Wire-Bound Wood Slats

Wire-bound wood slats provide a first-class, temporary solution for a problem spot that needs to be fenced. Time takes its toll on this lightweight material. The fencing is made of regularly spaced slats confined within a wire weft, and you can quickly and easily roll out an expanse of orderly picketlike pieces.

Wire-bound wood slats are commonly sold in lumberyards and home improvement centers. The style is often referred to as snow fencing, since that is its most typical application. It is quite inexpensive and is very easy to install.

Protection and security. Not very good. Suggests both but is not sturdy.

Visual privacy. Not very good.

Tempering the environment. Excellent for blocking drifting snow.

Defining space. Good for a temporary situation.

Suitable finish treatment. Let it weather naturally.

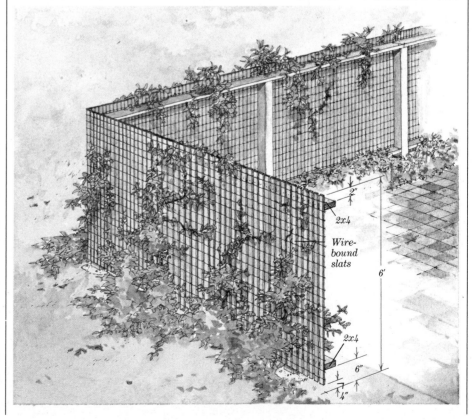

2"

2x4

Wire-bound slats

6'

2x4

6"

4"

Wire-Bound Reed

Wire-bound reed fencing is made from freshwater reeds woven every 4 inches with a weft of lightweight, noncorrosive wire. The feeling is exotic, so the fence might seem out of place in traditional surroundings. Because the reeds are flexible and easy to break or punch through, durability is not a strong point.

Home improvement centers and building supply outlets may carry wire-bound reed fencing, and it is inexpensive and easy to install.

Protection and security. Suggests both, but it is not sturdy.

Visual privacy. Very good. You can't see through it.

Tempering the environment. Good for blocking sun and drifting snow. Strong winds might tear it.

Defining space. Good, but seems temporary compared with most other types of fences.

Suitable finish treatment. Let it weather naturally.

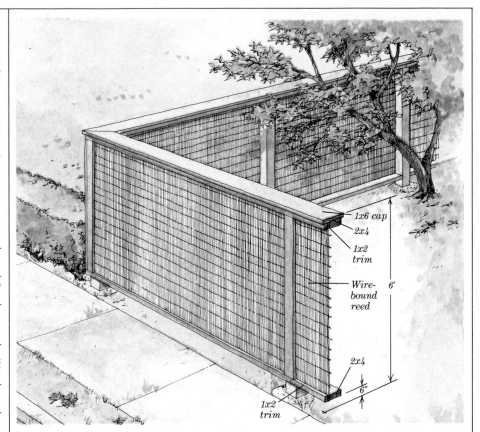

Wire-Bound Bamboo

Although similar in appearance to reed fencing, wire-bound bamboo is much stiffer. Bamboo has a color that is warm and soft, and the overall look can form an attractive backdrop for plantings.

This type of fencing may be found at home improvement centers and building supply centers. Wire-bound bamboo is very inexpensive and quick to install. Because it has some inherent structural strength and doesn't rot easily, it is fairly durable.

Protection and security. Moderate. It does not give a feeling of substance.

Visual privacy. Very good. You can't see through it.

Tempering the environment. Gives shade, softens wind, and blocks snow.

Defining space. Good. Gives a pleasant, informal feeling of closure.

Suitable finish treatment. Let it weather naturally.

Glass

A glass fence seems to be a conflict in terms. You can see through it, and you can break it to get in; but for some reason passersby also believe more in its function as a fence than in its vulnerability as glass. It can retain a view you especially like and protect your outdoor area from winds.

Glass is sold at glass outlets and is fairly expensive. For fences, use only tempered safety glass and have it professionally installed.

Protection and security. Good; provides more than it seems at first glance.

Visual privacy. Virtually none.

Tempering the environment. Blocks wind and drifting snow. Can buffer some noise, but not much.

Defining space. Good. It defines space without being a visual wall.

Suitable finish treatment. Finish only the frame. Paint, stain, or let it weather naturally.

Plastic and Fiberglass

Plastic and fiberglass are by nature synthetic, and thus are not always compatible with natural surroundings. But they can also form an interesting, clean-lined, pleasing contrast. They are sold at plastic and building supply outlets. The cost varies, depending on the thickness of the sheet. Installation is quick and easy.

Protection and security. Moderate to good, depending on the strength of the material.

Visual privacy. Very good. Translucent materials have the added advantage of admitting light.

Tempering the environment. Light comes in. Wind goes over the top, but may create downdrafts.

Defining space. Can be a light treatment that does not wall in a small area.

Suitable finish treatment. Finish only the frame. Paint, stain, or let it weather naturally.

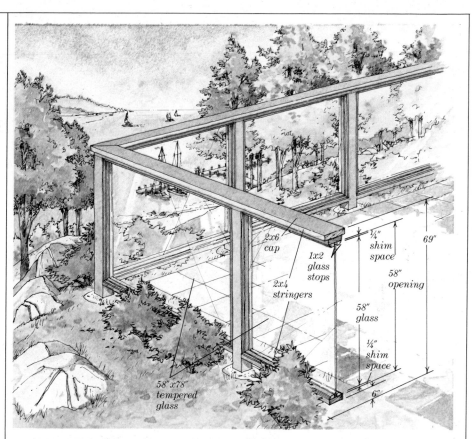

2x6 cap
1x2 glass stops
2x4 stringers
¼" shim space
69"
58" opening
58" glass
58" glass
¼" shim space
6"
58" x78" tempered glass

2x4 stringer
2x2 nailers
2x4
6'
Plastic
6"
4x4 intermediate mullion

Wire Mesh

Wire mesh is a very inexpensive and nice-looking way to get a lot of security and protection. The gridlike and rectilinear weaves of wire mesh are particularly attractive. Heavier materials have intersections of wire welded at the joint, making a rigid fabric that looks good for a long time.

Wire mesh is a common material and should be readily available at a lumberyard or building supply center. The cost is low and the construction time is short.

Protection and security. Excellent.

Visual privacy. None, unless you train climbing plants on it.

Tempering the environment. Will block drifting snow but little else.

Defining space. Defines space in a simple, functional way.

Suitable finish treatment. None is required.

Chain Link

Chain link fencing is popular for security, particularly in rough areas. It tends to look somewhat stark in garden settings, but special treatments can soften the strident metal look—wood insert slats, or vinyl-covered fencing for example. The materials are sold at home improvement centers and building supply outlets. Installation of chain link fences is not covered in this book.

Protection and security. Excellent. Chain link was designed for security.

Visual privacy. Generally none. With insert slats or plantings, moderate to good.

Tempering the environment. Can block drifting snow but little else.

Defining space. Defines space in a completely utilitarian way.

Suitable finish treatment. None is required.

Ornamental Iron

Ornamental iron is a classic fencing material. Most of today's ornamental iron work is fabricated with hollow steel tubing, rather than wrought iron. This type of fencing is pretty and sophisticated and requires just the right setting to be effective. It looks rich, light, and formal, and can range from a strongly vertical look to a wildly curly one, depending on the individual design. An ornamental iron fence should be designed and fabricated by a professional.

If you have your heart set on this kind of fence but find that the professional work is beyond the scope of your budget, you might want to explore the option of using prefabricated products designed for home installation. You can find them at home improvement centers and building supply outlets.

Protection and security. Very good if the fence is high enough and the infill pattern small enough.

Visual privacy. None.

Tempering the environment. May block drifting snow.

Defining space. Can work well. It is sometimes used for pool fencing.

Suitable finish treatment. Paint.

Variations

Virtually anything can be fabricated in metal—such is the nature of the material and the skill of a good smith. So design details and special elements that will make your ornamental iron fence ''just right'' are all within the domain of consideration. Many details are prefabricated parts that are specially sized and cast, and everything else can simply be made to order. Finials, twists, brass caps and fittings, curlicues, circles, and filigree sheets—these are but a few of the ways in which an ornamental iron fence gets its character.

Welded tubular steel

6'

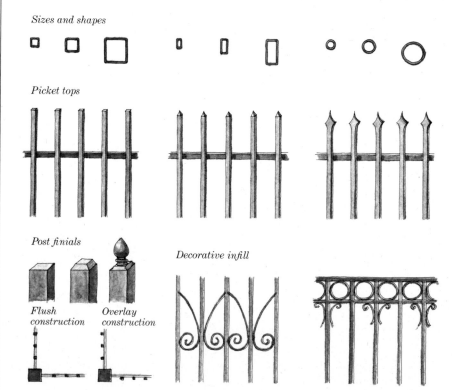

Sizes and shapes

Picket tops

Post finials

Flush construction   *Overlay construction*

Decorative infill

MAKING A BUILDING PLAN

No matter how different they might seem on the surface, fences are actually very much alike. Regardless of their style, fences are built according to the same construction sequence and are made from similar components.

Posts anchor the fence in the earth, stringers tie the posts together into a framework, and an infill material sheathes the frame, forming the fence surface and giving it structural strength.

Choosing a basic fence style entailed making decisions about your functional needs and aesthetic preferences. Making a building plan entails deciding how you will actually put the parts together to create the style you choose.

Although you're concerned with the entire fence, a fence is just a series of repeating *bays* (sections of fence from one post to the next), so you only need to consider the building details for one typical bay.

The fence styles illustrated on pages 26-41 provide typical fence designs, detail for detail. If you use one of those designs exactly as shown, skip to pages 50-55 to finalize the specifications you'll need for ordering materials and for building the fence. If you'd rather create a custom design, the next six pages illustrate alternative design and construction details that you might like to substitute. All the options are simply variations on a basic theme. Some assembly variations actually make building the fence easier, some produce a fence with greater strength, some simply make a prettier fence—and many other variations do all these things at once. Look them over to see which spark your interest or even inspire your own creations.

A Fence Is a Structural System

The illustration on the facing page shows the component parts of a fence—any fence. It is typical in every regard, so it's easy to see the structure that underlies the style. No matter how different two styles might look, the structural components remain the same: the footings, the framework, and the infill.

The following chart names the basic components, describes their purpose, points out their relationships, and suggests pages you might wish to refer to for a more detailed view of each. Use it to familiarize yourself with the fence as a structural system, so that when you review the alternative design and construction detail on the six pages that follow, you'll be able to consider their application in the style you've chosen to build.

Footings	The purpose of the footings is to keep the framework upright, stable, and securely rooted in the earth. The footing—no matter what type you choose (see page 53)—consists of the following component parts:
	Postholes. These should be dug with smooth, straight sides or better yet, with the sides slightly "undercut," so that the hole is wider at the bottom than at the top. To calibrate posthole diameters and depths, see the table on page 52. For how to dig postholes, see page 64.
	Filler. Filler is used to pack the hole and anchor the post to the earth once it has been positioned and braced. The illustration shows a concrete filler, though an earth-and-gravel mix or just plain earth can also be used to set the posts. See page 67 for filler details.
	Drainbed. The drainbed serves to support the post, and to allow rot-promoting groundwater to filter away from the base of the post. Here, a 6-inch gravel bed is used, and the post is embedded in it 2 inches so that concrete can't surround its base. Another way of creating a drainbed is to toss a large stone into the bottom of the hole to shield the base of the post from direct contact with earth. See pages 53 and 67 for further information.
Framework	The framework forms the structure to which the infill is fastened. Here, the framework shows a typical way of joining posts and stringers, but pages 44-47 offer you attractive alternatives, including special joints and stringer-to-post mounting positions. Any type of fence framework consists of the following components:
	Posts. The posts form the link to the earth. They should be set perfectly plumb and in proper alignment in order to do their job well. Page 52 offers you a summary of alternative post sizes and spacings. Pages 66-67 show you how to set the posts.
	Stringers. The stringers are the cross-members that join the posts to form the framework. They need to be cut to fit snugly post-to-post, and nailed securely in place. Pages 44-47 show you alternative ways of mounting stringers that negotiate a slope; pages 68-69 show you how to fit stringers and nail them to the posts.
Infill	The infill forms the actual fence surface. Pages 26-41 show you the range of materials and styles to choose from, and illustrate ways that infill can be mounted: on the face of the framework—nail-on style (as seen in the illustration at right), or inset to the frame. Pages 70-71 show you alternative approaches to infill placements, and pages 72-73 show you infill installation techniques.

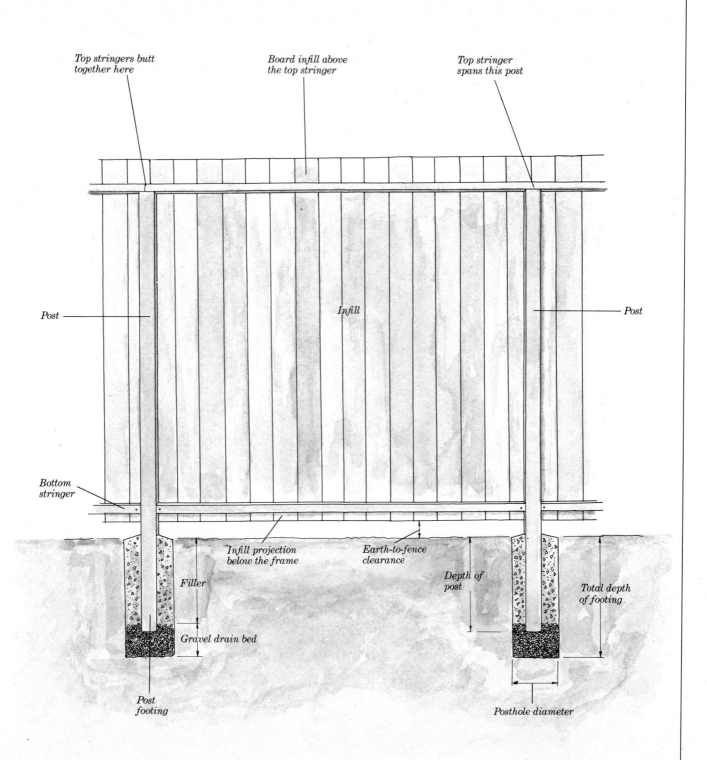

Top stringers butt together here

Board infill above the top stringer

Top stringer spans this post

Post

Infill

Post

Bottom stringer

Infill projection below the frame

Earth-to-fence clearance

Filler

Depth of post

Total depth of footing

Gravel drain bed

Post footing

Posthole diameter

Design and Construction Variations

The following six pages show you ways in which basic design and construction details, introduced in the preceding illustrations of fence styles, can be replaced with other ones. Look them over to see which ones you might choose to incorporate in your own custom fence design to improve its appearance, to increase its structural strength, or to give it a certain flair that will make it a specially pleasing project.

Change the Pallette

Wood materials come in a wide variety of sizes and shapes. Used in combination, those sizes and shapes create a unique visual rhythm and scale. Large structural members look bold and massive and can be softened and tailored by using smaller trim details. Smaller structural members look light and lacy and can be given extra visual weight by using cap pieces of a slightly larger scale.

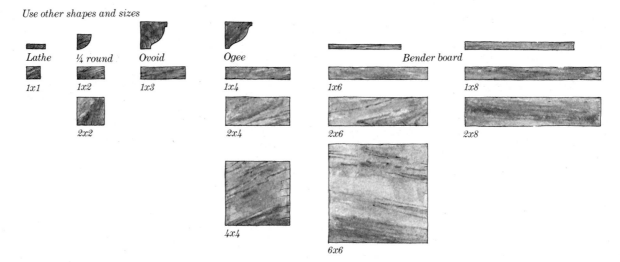

Use other shapes and sizes

Lathe   *¼ round*   *Ovoid*   *Ogee*   *Bender board*

1x1   1x2   1x3   1x4   1x6   1x8

2x2   2x4   2x6   2x8

4x4   6x6

Change the Joints

Housed joints, such as through-mortises, channel, and dado joints, are stronger than others, but they are also more difficult to make. Other joints, such as butt joints, are easier to make and are typically used for stringers. Miter joints are often used at corners, are pleasing to the eye, sufficiently strong, and fairly easy to construct.

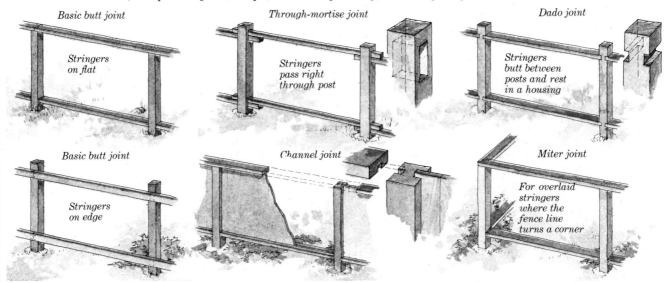

Basic butt joint
Stringers on flat

Through-mortise joint
Stringers pass right through post

Dado joint
Stringers butt between posts and rest in a housing

Basic butt joint
Stringers on edge

Channel joint

Miter joint
For overlaid stringers where the fence line turns a corner

Change the Stringer Position

Over long spans, or under heavy infill loads, 2 by 4 stringers mounted "on-flat" have a greater tendency to sag than stringers that are mounted "on-edge." For a view of the visual and structural effect of variations in post placement see the box on page 52.

Stringer Problems

Stringers on-flat have a greater tendency to sag since they are mounted on their thinner dimension, which is relatively flexible. Stringers on-edge are stiffer and have less tendency to sag over longer spans or under heavier loads.

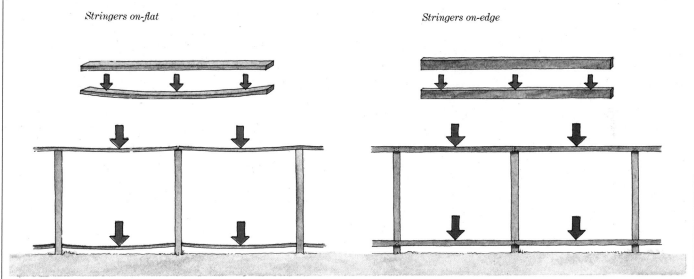

Stringers on-flat   Stringers on-edge

Stringer Solutions: Stringers On-Flat

If you are using 2 by 4 stringers on-flat over long spans, here are some ways to ensure a stiffer frame, one that isn't likely to sag. All of them are attractive approaches. Add a third stringer to share the infill load. Use wider stringers such as 2 by 6s with 6 by 6 posts. Use wider and thicker stringers such as 4 by 4s with 4 by 4 posts.

Add a third stringer to share the infill load

Use stringers of a wider dimension, such as 2x6s with 6x6 posts

Use stringers of a thicker dimension, such as 4x4s with 4x4 posts

Design and Construction Variations

Stringer Solutions: Stringers On-Edge

When stringers are mounted on-edge, you have a variety of choices for mounting the infill on the frame.

Stringers Centered on Post

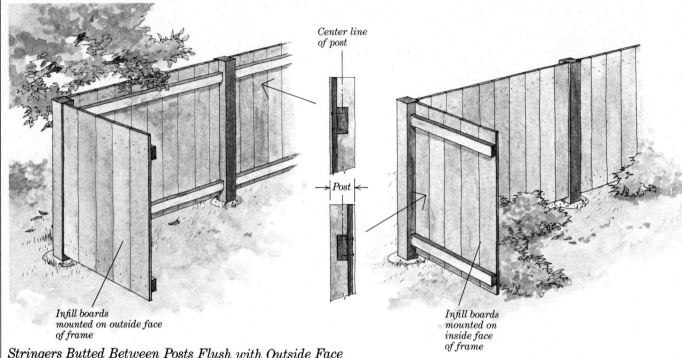

Center line of post

Post

Infill boards mounted on outside face of frame

Infill boards mounted on inside face of frame

Stringers Butted Between Posts Flush with Outside Face

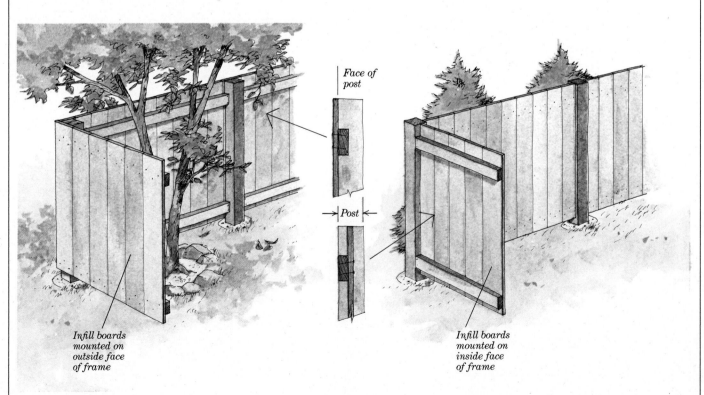

Face of post

Post

Infill boards mounted on outside face of frame

Infill boards mounted on inside face of frame

Stringers On-Edge Mounted on Outside Face of Posts

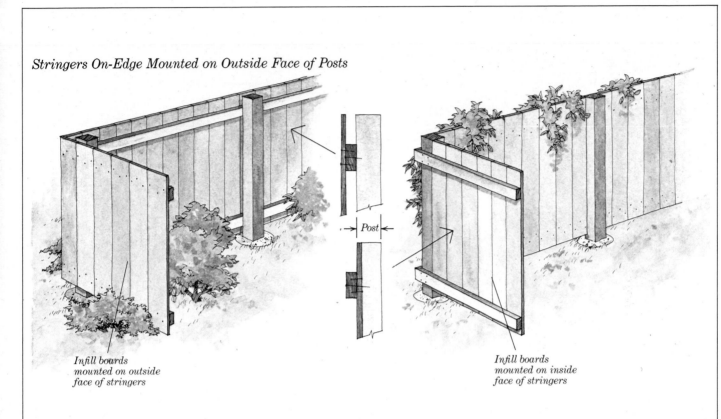

*Infill boards
mounted on outside
face of stringers*

Post

*Infill boards
mounted on inside
face of stringers*

Stringers On-Edge Mounted Bay by Bay on Alternating Sides of Posts

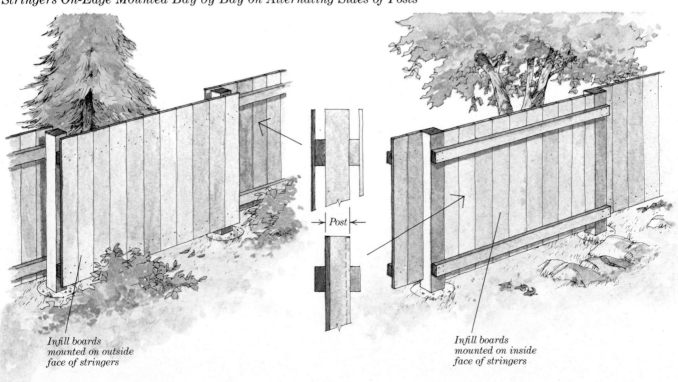

*Infill boards
mounted on outside
face of stringers*

Post

*Infill boards
mounted on inside
face of stringers*

Design and Construction Variations

Change the Fence Tops, Post Tops, and Caps

The details you choose to cap off your fence have a leading role to play. The top of the fence might not be the first thing you look at, but it's probably the first thing your eye actually *sees*—and one of the most vividly memorable. No matter how modest or elaborate, whimsical or simple, top edges are prominent aesthetic elements that capture your attention. See how the ideas below might cap off your own particular fence design.

The boards can cut a clean, straight line . . .

or have a special detail cut . . .

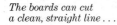

Pointed

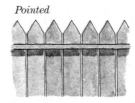

Dog-eared

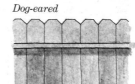

Filigree

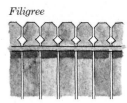

Scalloped

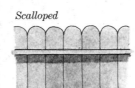

Saw-toothed

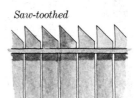

Picketed

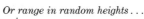

The tops can be beveled in succession to form a long, sweeping, concave curve . . .

Or range in random heights . . .

Or sit flush with the top of the stringer . . .

Or an extra-wide trim piece can cap off the edge.

The posts can project above the top stringers, with finials pointing skyward down the line

The posts can reach even higher to support a special border.

The border can be open and divided into proportional frames...

Or it can sport a contrasting infill all its own.

The fence can be arbored...

Or have a linear gable.

Dealing with Slopes and Obstructions

Sloped terrain presents a special set of conditions, both when you're planning your fence design and when you're building it. The illustrations below show you three ways in which the fence can negotiate a change in grade. If you don't know which type of framework will work best for your own situation, here's an easy way to find out: Gauge the slope and plot it out on paper. To experiment with alternatives, sketch them on paper.

Stepped Framework

In this approach, the frame itself remains rectilinear and each bay steps up the slope by an equal amount. It works best over gradual, even slopes. Any kind of board infill or sheet material such as plywood or preassembled panels of lattice works well with this type of fence framework. (Sheet materials should be mounted inset to the frame rather than overlying it in nail-on style.) The finished effect is crisp, classic, and architectural because the fence remains separate from the earth's slope rather than mirroring it.

Sloping Framework

In this style, each bay is framed to mirror the slope of the earth beneath it. The posts are plumb, but the stringers are mounted at an angle so that they parallel the grade. This approach is appropriate for almost any terrain—steep or gradual grades or uneven, rolling terrain. Posts and rails, narrow boards, slats, pickets, stakes, palings, and wirebound fencing all work well with this type of framework. Although nail-on styles work quite well, a sloped frame does not lend itself to infill that is inset to the frame.

Stepped Framework and Sloping Infill

This combination solution is often used on very steep grades. Under such conditions it is easier to build a stepped frame, but it leaves large triangular voids along the bottom of the fence and excessively large leaps of graduating rise at the top, which can look awkward and jarring. The solution is to mask them by extending the infill beyond the frame so that it follows the earth's contour.

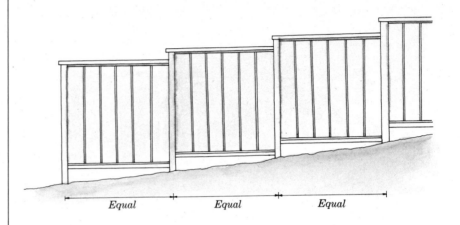

Equal   Equal   Equal

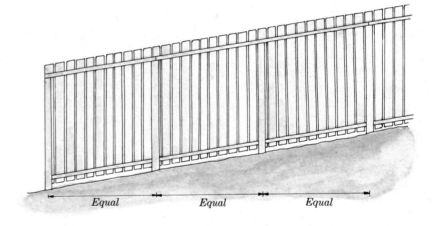

Equal   Equal   Equal

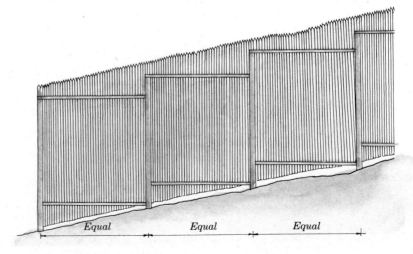

Equal   Equal   Equal

How to Gauge a Slope

The purpose of gauging a slope is two-fold. First, it helps you decide which of the three framework approaches you want to take. Second, it helps you determine how much each bay of a stepped frame must project above the one below it.

One way of gauging a slope is described here. There are others, but this is a typical one. Drive two stakes firmly into the earth (as shown in the illustration at right) and tie a string line to the top one. Wrap the other end of the string around a hand level. Move the assembly line up or down the stake until the string reads perfectly level.

Mark the point on the string where it crosses the stake, and mark the point on the stake where it is crossed by the string. To determine the "rise," measure from the earth to the mark on the stake; to determine the "run," measure the length of the string from stake to stake and write down both numbers. Use them to plot the slope on graph paper, and then sketch out framework approaches on a tissue overlay.

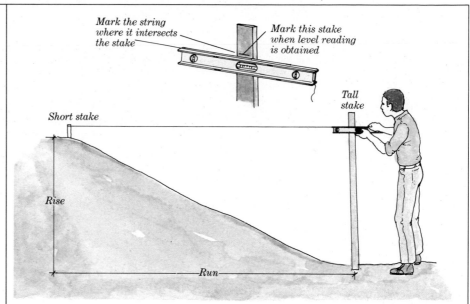

Mark the string where it intersects the stake

Mark this stake when level reading is obtained

Tall stake

Short stake

Rise

Run

How to Plot the Slope on Paper

Draw a baseline on your graph paper. Count the number of feet (boxes) of run and mark it. Next, count the number of feet or inches of rise and mark it. Connect the points, approximating the profile of the slope. Use tracing-paper overlays to experiment with and choose a framework approach for your fence.

If you choose a stepped frame, figure out how much each successive bay should step. Here's how:

1. Count the number of bays in the sloped section. (Your fence-line layout plan shows you. See page 54.)

2. Convert the slope's rise into inches; divide that figure by the number of bays. The result tells you the number of inches each bay needs to rise for the fence to step evenly.

Obstructions in the Fence Line

If your proposed fence line crosses paths with tree trunks, rock outcroppings, or gullies or swales, the fence will have to yield the right-of-way. The illustrations here offer a few standard approaches for dealing with such occurrences. (Note: If you had considered nailing the fencing—either frame or infill—to the trunk of a tree, be aware that the tree may not be able to survive. Puncture wounds subject the living tree to bacterial invasion and generally disturb the flow of life. Even posts placed too close to a tree can destroy its root system, and the tree can die as a result. Reposition the fence line or stop it short of the tree so that the tree can continue to grow.)

Complete Your Plan

Whether you selected a ready-made fence design from pages 26-41 or used one as a basis for your own custom design, there are two things to do before your plan is completed. One is to choose a footing—the way in which you'll root the fence in the earth (see the illustrated comparison of footing types to decide which one will work best for you). The other is to divide the fence-line layout plan into bays. If you're using a specified design from the fence style section, simply follow the guidelines for dividing up the line given on the facing page. If you've developed a custom design, take a look at the "Post Sizes and Spacing" box to see what some of your options are. If your property slopes, or if there are obstructions in the fence line, the preceding two pages show you the standard ways in which a fence can negotiate these conditions. They probably won't alter your plan, so you can go ahead and complete it, although when you purchase materials and actually build the fence, these unique sections will be treated a little differently.

At this stage in your planning, it might be useful to have a look at the chapter on gates (pages 79-93). Though you needn't make detailed decisions about individual gates in order to complete your plan, you'll want to be sure that the size of gate openings and their placement in the fence line is just right before you divide the fence line into bays.

Look over the information and instructions on these two pages, and capture your ideas on paper, in every detail. A sketch of one typical bay gives you the chance to preview the whole, to troubleshoot potential problems, and to confirm the workability of your plan. It also helps you discover questions that might require special advice. With the help of this sketch and your fence-line layout plan, your materials supplier can help determine how much material you'll need, and will figure out the most efficient way to purchase the stock so that cut-off waste is minimized.

Post Sizes and Spacing

Post sizes and spacing are more than just structural issues—they're also aesthetic ones. The frame itself (posts and stringers) creates a visual rhythm. That rhythm can be so pleasing and so much a part of the fence design that what is often considered the back side of the fence can easily be more beautiful than the front—it all depends on your perspective!

What size, and how far apart, should the posts be? The table below can guide your own decisions, but keep in mind that, visual considerations aside, posts play a key structural role.

Gate posts, end posts, and corner posts (all of which are called terminal posts) have the heaviest job to do, since they have nothing to hang on to except the earth itself. Terminal posts should be set deeper (see the footings chart), and be dimensioned one size larger than line posts (those that fall in between). Also, note that the farther apart the posts are, the sturdier the stringers must be, so that they can resist the tendency to sag.

4 by 4 Posts at 6 Feet On-Center. This is a tight spacing that bears a heavy infill load well, looks sturdy, and is nicely proportioned for both tall and low fencing. This spacing carries the eye along the fence at a sprightly pace.

4 by 4 Posts at 8 Feet On-Center. This is a typical spacing that works well for lighter-weight infill, unless the stringers are mounted on edge, which is a sturdier position than mounted on flat. (See pages 44-47 for alternative stringer positions.) This spacing will move the eye down the fence line at an average, gentle pace.

6 by 6 Posts at 8 Feet On-Center. This is a strong spacing, both visually and structurally. The size of the posts is handsomely massive, but the distance between them interjects a pleasing grace. The eye goes down the fence line at a calm pace and enjoys the beauty of the framework.

6 by 6 Posts at 10 Feet On-Center. For members of such large dimensions, 10 feet is an average spacing in terms of strength. But the generous distance between posts gives an expansive quality. Stringers should be made of 2 by 6 stock to bridge the spans with appropriate strength. This spacing moves the eye smoothly down the fence line with a rest in each bay.

About Footings and Frost Heave

If you live in a region where frost heave occurs, pay heed to the advice of local experts in the art of fence building. This is the problem that nature has dealt: Water expands when it freezes; this causes the earth to heave, which tends to push posts out of alignment and out of their post holes in the process. In some regions, earth-and-gravel backfill footings are the common choice, since this type of footing keeps water away from the post rather than holding it there. In other regions, builders advocate using concrete post footings for exactly the same reasons! If you don't have a strong feeling about which type to use, call a local materials supplier or a fencing contractor to learn what experience has taught them about the best footing to use under your specific conditions.

Earth-and-gravel backfill has been used for centuries to keep fences of every style upright and firmly planted in the earth. They work best where soils are essentially stable; they tend to lose their grip in soils that slide or crack due to a heavy clay content, or in very light soils that cannot resist the lateral loads of wind and weather.

If your soil conditions aren't the recommended ones, but the fence is low (or tall but fairly lightweight or open), an earth-and-gravel backfill footing will probably be just fine for line posts. Terminal posts—and particularly gate posts—are best set in concrete.

Concrete post footings are generally recommended for any type of fencing of any height in any type of soil. They maintain the stability of the fence very well. The footing itself increases the area of the post's bearing surface against the earth, which helps secure and firmly root the fence despite the weather and wear it faces. Also, because the post is not in direct contact with the earth, a concrete post footing reduces the post's tendency to rot. Here, however, a big proviso: Concrete protects the post against rot, provided the bottom of the post is *not* encased in concrete—but instead embedded 2 inches deep in a 6-inch bed of gravel. This ensures optimum drainage. If concrete caps the bottom of the post, water will collect there and the post will rot.

Choose a Footing

Two types of footing are commonly used in fence construction: earth-and-gravel backfill and concrete post footings. Each type works a little differently and serves best under different sets of conditions. Those conditions organize themselves around these issues: the type of soil, the climate, the height and weight of the fence, and the type of post (line or terminal). Your own set of conditions might be unique, and if you have questions about which type of footing will be best for your situation, your materials supplier can give you special guidance. Regional building techniques earn their place in tradition by successful trial over time.

Earth-and-Gravel Backfill   Concrete Post Footings

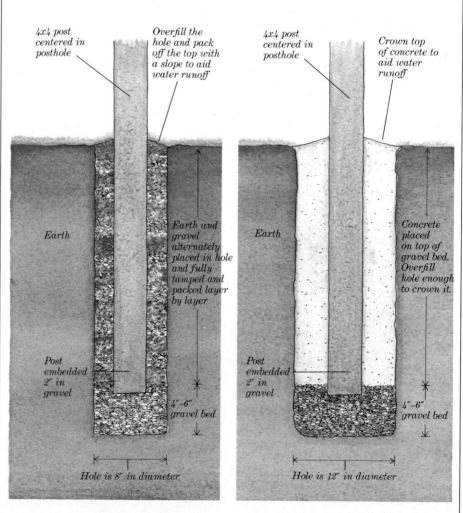

4x4 post centered in posthole

Overfill the hole and pack off the top with a slope to aid water runoff

Earth

Earth and gravel alternately placed in hole and fully tamped and packed layer by layer

Post embedded 2" in gravel

4"–6" gravel bed

Hole is 8" in diameter

4x4 post centered in posthole

Crown top of concrete to aid water runoff

Earth

Concrete placed on top of gravel bed. Overfill hole enough to crown it.

Post embedded 2" in gravel

4"–6" gravel bed

Hole is 12" in diameter

Dividing the Fence Line into Bays

Dividing the fence line into bays is a process of marrying an aesthetic point of view with a technical one. When you decided where to put the fence (pages 20-23), you may have had a specific post spacing in mind and adhered to it—in which case simply mark the post locations on your plan. If post spacing wasn't your primary concern, this is how to divide the fence line into bays.

Make a Quick Computation
Pick a section of the fence line (from one terminal post to the next) and divide it by the on-center post spacing you want. Do you wind up with a remainder—an odd-sized bay? It's a pretty sure bet you will, but there are three ways to deal with it. All of them are right, so use the one that works best for you.

1. Shorten or lengthen that section of fence line to get rid of the odd-sized bay.

2. Split the remainder in half and assign the extra length to the two end bays in that section. The bays will be symmetrically harmonious, even though they're odd-sized.

3. Change your post spacing so that each bay in that section absorbs the remainder in equal measure.

Before you decide which solution to use, compute the division for each section of the fence line; you might see a pattern of remainders that will tell you the easiest approach to take.

Post Spacings

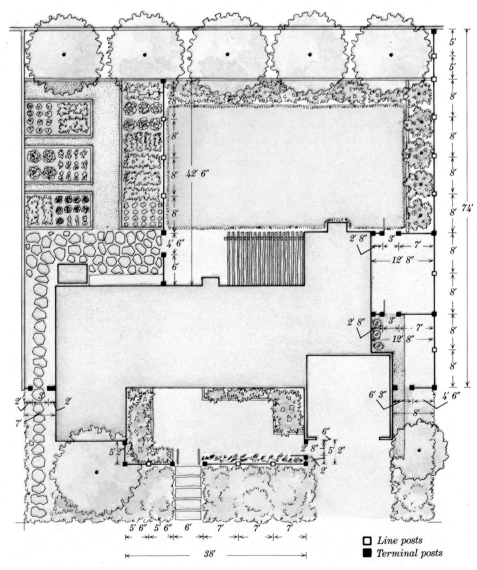

☐ Line posts
■ Terminal posts

Also, note that different sections of the fence line can have their own post spacings without creating a chaotic visual effect as long as the differences between them are discreet.

When you've divided the fence line into bays, note the post locations on your plan. Use solid black boxes to indicate terminal posts and open boxes to indicate line posts. Write in the dimensions of the bays. This information tells you how many posts you need and the length of each bay. It also provides a layout plan.

Sketch a Bay

Sketching one bay in detail provides you and your supplier with exact dimensions of each component of the fence. Here's how to make the sketch: Tape a piece of tracing paper over a sheet of graph paper, and sketch in a baseline to represent the earth. Plot out the posts, the stringers, and the footings, letting 1 inch equal 1 foot.

Then tape a sheet of tracing paper over this one, and sketch in the infill and any special details. (This way, if you need to make erasures, the framework remains intact.)

When all the parts are in place, trace the information from the bottom sheet onto the top one so that the whole drawing is on the same page. Then assign dimensions to each component of the fence, and to the overall height and width of the bay, so that every aspect of the plan is defined, sized, and dimensioned.

Final Fence Design

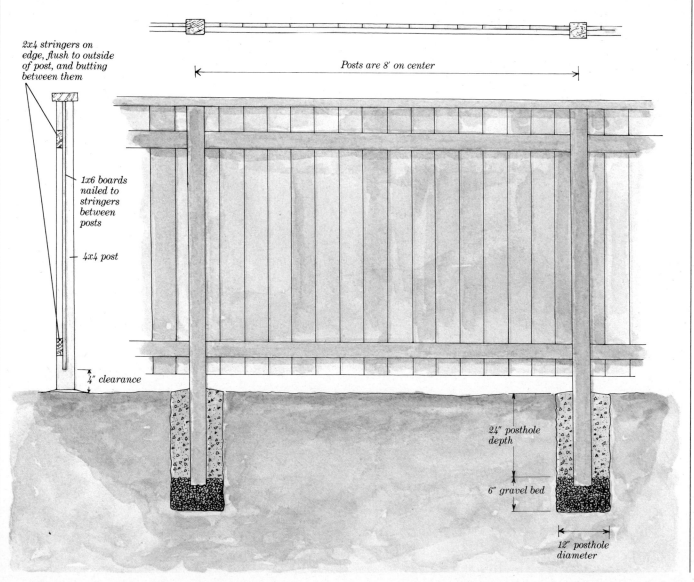

2x4 stringers on edge, flush to outside of post, and butting between them

Posts are 8' on center

1x6 boards nailed to stringers between posts

4x4 post

4" clearance

24" posthole depth

6" gravel bed

12" posthole diameter

GETTING READY TO BUILD

*F*ence building is a straightforward process that consists of three basic phases. Each phase uses a different set of skills and tools. Some of them you might already have, and those you don't have can be acquired fairly easily.

You don't have to do all the work yourself in order to enjoy the satisfaction of having designed and built your fence. Instead, you might like to explore the possibility of contracting out part or all of the installation work.

Before you decide on an approach, consider the project in terms of budget. The dollar outlay for materials is the most tangible form of expense. But your own time and energy are also important parts of the total cost.

How much time do you plan to spend? A week's vacation? A few successive weekends? Or are after-work hours the only free times you can devote to building the fence?

And what about your skills? Each phase of the work calls for a particular set of skills. Some might be easy for you, but others might seem like drudgery. It might be worthwhile for you to save your time and energy for the parts you really enjoy and pay someone else to do the parts you can't handle easily.

Working With Professionals

The telephone directory or the "Services" columns in your newspaper's classified section can provide the names of contractors who can help build your fence, and a few quick telephone conversations will start the process moving.

The first step is to describe the nature and extent of your project—how many postholes need to be dug, for instance, or how many square feet of fence need to be painted.

The next step is to invite bids from those contractors that seem promising to you. To do this, they need to visit the site, and get a closer look at the details of the project. Then they can give you a firmer idea of cost and scheduling, and prepare a bid.

If you accept a bid, ask for a contract clearly detailing the work to be done, the time period in which it is to be completed, the quality of materials to be used, and the fee for each phase of the work. The purpose of the contract is to protect both parties; that protection is created by arriving at a shared understanding of the responsibilities of each one. It is a helpful document that frees you both to find satisfaction in the deal.

Phasing the Work

The Groundwork
• Staking the layout
• Digging the holes

Layout is an easily acquired skill, but it is much easier to do with an additional set of hands. The layout must be done carefully and accurately if the fence is to come out well aligned and true.

If your plan calls for lots of fencing, you will need lots of postholes. How many holes can you dig by hand and still maintain enthusiasm? Probably about a dozen. Power-driven augers can be rented, but keep in mind that they generate lot of torque—so much so, in fact, that they can toss you around quite a bit. And a 12-inch-diameter auger needs two strong people to operate it.

You can hire out the work to the types of firms listed below. A posthole-drilling contractor may or may not be willing to stake the layout first, but the other types of firms generally do that as part of the job. If you'd like to have the posts set as well, ask whether that task can be included as part of the job they bid.

Contractors. Drilling contractor, landscape contractor, fence contractor, builder, handyperson.

The Assembly
• Setting the posts
• Installing the infill
• Completing the trim details

The assembly phase requires basic building skills, and a fence project is a good way to develop them. The most exacting step is setting the posts (see notes on groundwork) because it establishes the foundation and framework for the fence. This is much easier to do in teams of two people. Each post needs to be plumbed, aligned, and braced. Then, hole after hole, the mixed batch of concrete must be "poured," or the earth-and-gravel backfill must be placed and fully tamped.

Installing the stringers, the infill, and the trim details is fun to do, fast, and easy; you see the product of your efforts take shape before your eyes.

If you're not confident about your ability to measure, cut, and nail with sufficient accuracy, you'll learn how if you do this phase. Should you choose not to do this yourself, your options for hire are listed below.

Contractors. Landscape contractor, fence contractor, lumberyard installation service, handyperson.

The Finish
• Preparing surfaces
• Applying sealers, primers, and paints

Applying surface finishes takes time and skill to do a good job—one that will look good and last. Many people find this a pleasant pastime; others consider it a chore. You might find this a relaxing kind of work and quite satisfying for the transformation it brings—the finishing touch. If it's not your preference, a painter can do the job in short order, applying all three coats—one prime coat and two finish coats. The finish can be rolled on and brushed out, brushed on, or sprayed on with an airless sprayer on a *very* still day (the paint mist can travel onto your own or your neighbors' property and stick there).

Contractors. Painter, handyperson.

Finishes

Surface finishes have a wonderful way of transforming a lot of little pieces into a unity of parts—a single element that blends with the whole site design. Because the finish you choose might affect the type of material you purchase, it's best to think about finishes at this stage of your planning.

Stains and paints give the fence protection and certainly transform its appearance as well. Sealers don't appreciably change its appearance, but they do give protection. Bleaches, on the other hand, give no protection but they change the look by speeding up natural weathering processes and lightening the natural wood tones.

As you consider surface finish treatments, you will want to focus on color, tone, and surface sheen (from flat to glossy), degree of durability and of protection, and ease of application. You'll also want to make sure that products are compatible with one another and with the fence material itself, and that they are within your budget. Your materials supplier will be able to help you choose finish products.

Sealers	Sealers are clear finishes that seal the wood against water penetration without altering its color. Exposure to the elements will eventually weather any wood material to gray, but sealers slow the process. *Used with bleaches.* Sealers keep bleaches from taking effect unless you wait about two months after applying the sealer, and then apply the bleaching agent. *Used under stains and paints.* For very porous woods, sealer can be used under a primed and painted finish for extra protection. Make sure the products you use are compatible with each other.
Primers	Paints won't stick to raw wood without the help of a primer. Primers actually penetrate the wood's surface and provide some *tooth* so the paint will stay bonded to it. Primers also make paint application faster. *Oil-based primers.* Oil-based primers penetrate and adhere to the wood more fully than do water-based primers. They need to be thinned with solvents, so they're more trouble to clean up. (Redwood and red cedar have extractives that tend to dissolve and bleed through the paint coat. The best insurance against this is to *always* use an oil-based—never a water-based—primer. Even then it's best to test a sample of primer on a scrap of material and expose it to the weather for about a week.) *Water-based primers.* Water-based primers provide an effective undercoat, and are easy to clean up. They are less expensive than oil-based products but are not compatible with redwood or red cedar.
Paints	Paints look clean, crisp, fresh, and architectural and are an appealing counterpoint to natural surroundings, especially if they borrow the color themes of the dwelling. Painted finishes tend to last longer and look better on surfaced fencing materials than on rough-sawn ones. Because paints form an opaque film on the surface of the wood, they can conceal defects in lower-grade lumber and still create a very handsome finished effect, an advantage that stains can't offer. They can also be periodically recoated. However, paints are more expensive and require more care in application. *Types of paint.* There are two broad categories of paints to choose from: exterior alkyds, which are oil-based products (durable and more costly), and exterior latex paints, which are water-based (less durable and less expensive). Each category offers a range of colors and surface sheens (gloss, semigloss, and flat or matte).
Stains	Stains have a blander finished effect than paints, but they allow a fence to harmonize with both the landscape and the architecture. Stains are easier to apply than paints because they require no undercoat. They go on easily over both rough- and smooth-surfaced materials. Semitransparent stains are particularly suitable for highlighting the beauty of wood grains. Heavy-bodied stains resemble paints in their opacity, but because stains penetrate the wood's surface (rather than forming a layer over it) they cannot actually conceal defects. Stains are somewhat less expensive than paints and take less time to apply. *Types of stains.* Stains come in two broad categories: water-based and oil-based. Each category offers differences in opacity, ability to penetrate the wood's surface, durability, and cost (depending on the composition). Stains don't offer much choice in surface sheen; they tend to retain the wood's natural look. *Color.* Heavy-bodied stains contain more pigments and generally emulate the effects of paint more fully than the light-bodied stains do. Light-bodied stains have fewer pigments, are more transparent, and tend to wear away more quickly than heavy-bodied stains. If you just want to quick-weather the fence, use a stain that matches that kind of wood when it's weathered. As the stain wears off, the wood will have weathered and the differences won't be very apparent. Make sure products are compatible with one another and with the wood. Note that pressure-treated lumber products have been treated with a chemical agent that can affect the color of the stain.
Bleaches	Bleaches offer an intermediate solution to the jarring look of a brand-new fence. They soften the raw wood look and blend the fence in quickly—as nature would have done after a season or two. Bleaches work by interacting with the elements. Some products might be harmful to your garden—a fact that you will need to consider. Because sealers inhibit bleaching action, be sure to read the section on sealers above.

Choosing Lumber

If you haven't yet chosen a specific type of lumber for your new fence, selecting it is simply a matter of reviewing the range of options and narrowing your selection down to one or two of them. That seems easy enough (and it is), but the range is wide and there are several avenues of approach you might take.

Your options largely depend on what is locally sold and available to you. Lumber is somewhat regionally specific in that it is shipped to locations where it will sell and where market demand is closely tied to local building traditions. The materials and techniques used for construction in your area have earned their popularity by trial over a period of time. They can be trusted to work. But your choice needn't be limited to these traditions if other types of materials or techniques seem better to you.

The list below outlines basic issues that come up when considering building materials for your fence:

- Availability
- Performance
- Longevity
- Durability
- Cost
- Appearance
  —grain patterns
  —surface texture
  —natural color
- Finish possibilities
- Workability
- Climate
- Toxicity

Some of these considerations will be important to you; others won't. Cost, appearance, and performance are generally the most prevalent concerns, though you'll decide which matter most to you.

Are You Chiefly Concerned With Cost?

You'll want to find the best quality material within your budget. A simple fence can require a sizable expenditure, though careful shopping and negotiating can be worth the effort. The information here can help you compare differences in cost for the kind of fence you're planning.

Is Appearance the Most Important Element?

If you want to match your home's exterior, an existing fence, or some other outdoor construction in color, texture, and grain, your options are narrowed considerably. (If your design calls for a particular surface finish, make sure the lumber is compatible with it.) See the chart on the previous page for more information.

Is Durability the Key Issue?

Building a fence takes some time and energy. You might be most interested in the durability of the material so you won't have to mend it because the materials rotted out. The section that follows discusses performance.

Wood Materials and Products

Wood materials are subject to decay—it is a fact of nature. And yet some species—*but only the heartwood sections of those species*—are naturally able to resist decay and insects. Redwood, cedar, cypress, and locust are perhaps the most commonly milled woods of this rot-resistant category. The heartwood sections of these trees are naturally saturated with resins that make the wood fibers useless as food for fungi and termites.

Because of their workability, their appreciable beauty, and their longevity—and their relative scarcity—these species are more costly than other softwood species, which are good building products but offer no *natural* resistance to decay.

An industrial chemical process simulates this natural state of resistance-to-decay by forcing preservatives deep into the wood fibers. Some common inexpensive softwood species (pine, hemlock, spruce, fir, etc.) are rendered decay-resistant in this way. These products are known as *pressure-treated lumber*. They are not classified by species and grade but are categorized according to

their uses: above-grade uses or below-grade uses. Pressure-treated lumber products are substantially less expensive than the naturally decay-resistant species; and their longevity, regardless of climate, is remarkable—40 years is a good average.

Why would anyone choose a more expensive material for outdoor construction when the less expensive ones have similar merits? There are many reasons: in order to match the new fence to existing outdoor building materials; out of a preference for the grain patterns, texture, weathering or finishing qualities; because of concerns about toxins leaching out of the material and into the earth; for local availability; or a regard for tradition. Some of these reasons might apply to your situation.

Species and treatments aside, there is also the issue of climate. Some regions have such dry climates that virtually any softwood, whether it's decay-resistant or not, can be used for outdoor construction with little likelihood of rot. Other regions are so humid and wet that the processes of deterioration are accelerated.

Wood Preservatives

Wood that has no natural resistance to decay (such as pine, fir, hemlock, and spruce) needs a shell of protection if it is exposed to the weather. Various toxic materials, called wood preservatives, can be applied to lumber to provide this shell of protection, though their effectiveness is questioned. The most effective method of application is by pressure treatment. Many preservatives that were formerly used for at-home applications are no longer available to homeowners or anyone else without a state applicator license, since they have been banned from over-the-counter sales by the Environmental Protection Agency.

Plywood

Plywood, like lumber, is produced in a variety of sizes, thicknesses, textures, species, and grades. Any plywood used for outdoor construction must be an exterior-grade material—fabricated with glues that will not deteriorate when exposed to moisture—so that the sheet will stay flat and veneers will stay tightly bonded.

Use AA exterior grades for sheathing that will be stained or painted or seen from both sides. Any surface defects (such as knots that have been plugged and touch-sanded) will show through the finish and detract from the appearance. A lesser grade will be just fine for sheathing that will be covered with some other material, such as shingles.

Remember that fences take a lot of wear and tear from the elements. Wind in particular puts a lateral load on both the framework and the infill. Plywood is stiff and rigid; the thicker the material, the greater its rigidity, which will keep the fence looking flat, smooth, and crisply architectural.

Shop by Sight

The best way to get a sense of which materials are right for your project is to take an exploratory trip to the lumberyard. Look at the different species, at their color and grain patterns. Check out quality differences between grades. Note how rough-sawn material differs in appearance and size from surfaced lumber. Look at pressure-treated products.

If you don't have a good idea of what you'd like to use, take your fence-line layout and elevation sketch with you and ask a salesperson to give you appropriate recommendations and an idea of costs. Then take a second look. Get your hands on some lumber; go through the racks and check a piece for defects. *Sight down its length on both the flat side and the edge.* Is it crooked? Warped? Or nicely flat? *Check for knots.* Are they small or tight? Loose and large? *Look for checks and splits.* More will naturally develop as the lumber seasons (unless its kiln-dried).

Compare Quality and Cost

When you have the issues sorted out and have a good idea of the material you want to use, shop around to get a comparison of materials and costs. You might find that a higher-grade material costs less at one yard than a lower grade at another.

Nominal Dimensions and Actual Dimensions

The dimensions used to describe a piece of lumber—1 by 4, 2 by 4, 6 by 6, and so forth—are its *nominal dimensions.* They name the thickness and width of the stock but don't describe its actual size. A piece of surfaced lumber is actually thinner and narrower than its nominal dimensions indicate. For example, a 1 by 4 actually measures ¾ inch by 3½ inches, a 2 by 4 actually measures 1½ inches by 3½ inches, and so on. These differences are a result of the surfacing or milling process.

Reductions in size from nominal dimensions to actual ones are consistently standard, but if size is particularly significant to your design, you might want to measure actual board dimensions. For example, if you've planned a rough-sawn 1-by-6 board infill with spaces between them, to be inset to the frame, you'll want to know exactly how many boards, and the size of the spaces, it would actually take to complete a bay.

Nails

You'll need to select the right size and type of nails for your project. Although nails come in a wide variety, they narrow to just a few that are typically used for fence construction.

First, the type of metal used to fabricate the nail is an important consideration. Some nails rust readily, and others won't ever rust. Those that do rust will leave dark stains on the fence surface, produce rust stains that bleed indelibly through a pristine coat of paint, and generally weaken the nail's ability to function, which ultimately weakens the entire fence.

Choose a type of metal that suits your fence treatment. Steel nails rust, but they are the least expensive. Hot-dipped galvanized nails resist rust fairly well (though eventually they will succumb to corrosion), and they cost a little more. Aluminum nails are a fine choice for a painted fence. Copper, brass, bronze, and stainless steel also do not rust; they are also the most expensive, and can be hard to find. Although special styles of infill might require special nail sizes and shapes, typically successful ones are described below.

- Common nails: for the frame— 2-by stock or thicker (16d)
- Box nails: for the infill—1-by stock or thinner (8d or 10d)
- Finish nails: for the fine trim details (6d or 8d)

Each of these specifications describes a particular shape. (For instance, common nails look different from finish nails. They work differently as well.) The specifications also describe the shank's diameter and length.

A special type called a *duplex nail* will come in handy during installation as a temporary fastener. Duplex nails have a double head; this makes it easy to pull them when you strip away braces, but the primary head will seat the nail tightly while you want the brace in place. You will need a pair per brace, but buy twice as many as you think you need to allow for bent or lost nails.

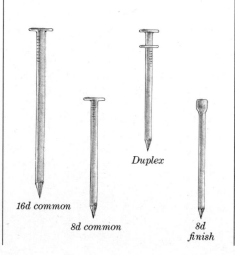

16d common

8d common

Duplex

8d finish

Estimating Costs and Preparing Materials

If you'd like to estimate your materials costs at home, you'll need some current price books, or the names of a few materials suppliers and a telephone close at hand. It should take only a couple of hours to figure it out from scratch.

On the other hand, if you'd like to get a quick idea of what the costs might be, here's an easy way to do it. Call a lumberyard and ask a salesperson to give you the materials cost for the basic style of fence you're planning to install. You'll need to provide the basic information (see one example below).

Fence style—Nail-on board fence with a 1-by-6 board infill.

Width and height of the bay—Posts are 7 feet on center; each bay has 2 stringers; the fence is 6 feet tall.

Species of wood you want to use—First choice, surfaced cedar; second choice, redwood.

Type of footing—Concrete post footings with posts set 30 inches deep.

Finish treatment—None; it will weather naturally.

The salesperson can probably compute the cost for you right there in a rough estimate form, or return your call later with the answer. You needn't hesitate to ask for this computation. Your call represents an opportunity to provide the service that salespeople are in business for, and most often they're happy to do it.

Placing the Lumber Order

To place an order, you'll need to be able to specify exactly the material you want, with all its details of classification and category. Besides species and grades, which are summarized below, the other set of specifications you make in placing the lumber order is the material dimension—the thicknesses, widths, and lengths of each of the various parts. A 2 by 4 by 16', for example, might describe the dimensions of a stringer, if you plan to have them span 3 posts.

Species of wood describes the natural characteristics of strength, color,

grain pattern, weathering traits, finishing characteristics, and ability to resist decay.

Grade of material describes the type and number of defects (knots, checks, etc.) that you can expect to encounter. These defects affect the material's performance and its cost. Grading systems vary for different species.

Appearance describes the type of milling treatments the material has had: rough-sawn, surfaced smooth, or hand-split.

Seasoning describes how "green" the material is—how much moisture has been given up, and therefore how much it can be expected to shrink or change shape as it dries.

Dimensions describe the size, in this order: thickness, width, and length (e.g., a 1 by 4, 10 feet long).

For pressure-treated materials, many of these categories are included in the general category of pressure-treated lumber. But you will have to specify the projected use as either above ground (infill, stringers, trim) or below ground (posts).

You will find that you can negotiate a better price for your materials if you place the full order with one lumberyard. You might like to have them deliver the load as well. This approach can save you time and money, and the salesperson can help you figure out all the materials and supplies you need so that you don't find yourself short.

Guidelines for Postholes and Footings

These rules of thumb form the basis for your footing design. These guidelines are based on average weather conditions and a typical board fence. If your own situation doesn't fit, consult your materials supplier for special advice.

Earth-and-Gravel Backfill
Minimum posthole diameter. The posthole diameter should be at least 2 times the width of the post, for example:
• 4-by-4 post: 8 inches diameter
• 6-by-6 post: 12 inches diameter
Minimum posthole depth. The total posthole depth is based on the sum of two amounts. For *line posts:*

1. Divide the total aboveground height of the fence (including infill) by 3.

2. To that figure, add an extra 6 inches of depth for the rock or gravel bed.

For terminal posts, add an extra foot to the total posthole depth.
Materials Needed to Set the Posts. You will need about ½ cubic foot of gravel for the 6-inch bed at the bottom of the hole. The earth and gravel mix used for backfill will require another 1½ cubic feet (2 cubic feet per hole should be ample).

Concrete Post Footings
Minimum posthole diameter. The posthole diameter should be at least 3 times the width of the post. For example:
• 4-by-4 post: 12 inches diameter
• 6-by-6 post: 18 inches diameter
Minimum posthole depth. The total posthole depth is based on the sum of two amounts. For *line posts:*

1. Divide the total aboveground height of the fence (including infill) by 3.

2. To that figure, add an extra 6 inches of depth for the rock or gravel bed.

For terminal posts, add an extra foot to the total posthole depth.
Materials Needed to Set the Posts. You will need about ½ cubic foot of gravel for the 6-inch bed at the bottom of the hole. You will also need approximately 1 bag of premixed fence concrete per hole (or ⅔ cubic foot of mixed concrete) for line posts, and more for terminal posts (which are set deeper).

Storage and Handling

Lumber materials should be protected from exposure to direct sunlight or moisture before they are installed. (After installation, these conditions pose no problems because the pieces are tightly joined; but before that, sunlight and moisture will cause them to twist, warp, cup, and develop defects unnecessarily.)

Wood materials have a certain moisture content when they're purchased. Unless they were purchased kiln-dried, they will still be undergoing the process of drying. This needs to happen gradually and evenly if they are to season properly. Stack them carefully (in filtered light or in the shade or under cover) so that they are flat and evenly weighted, with space between each piece to allow air to circulate.

Preinstallation Prep Work

Depending on the type of finish treatment you're planning, you might choose to do the prep work before you install the fence. Since you can prepare most of the materials all at once before they're assembled, these steps are faster and easier at this stage.

Applying Water-Repellent Sealers

Stack 4 by 4s together to form a trough large enough to hold your longest pieces of material. Line the trough with a couple of full-size thicknesses of heavy-duty plastic sheeting. Fill the trough with the water-repellant sealer and put all the materials through the bath. Lean them against a wall on end to dry, or carefully stack them log-cabin style.

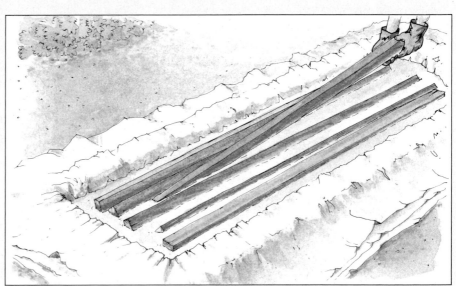

Applying Primer

Set out a pair of sawhorses on a piece of plastic sheeting. Then lay a batch of lumber down on them. Roll on a coat of primer to exposed surfaces. When they're dry, flip the batch over and do the other side and the edges until all the surfaces are primed. Lean the batch up on end against a wall to dry, and repeat the process until all your material is primed and ready to go.

Installation begins with staking the layout, the point at which your plans leave the paper and get down to earth. It consists of two phases.

First, you will install a pair of batter boards for each section of the fence line (see the facing page). Second, you will stretch a string line taut between each pair of batter boards, check their positions, and then adjust them accordingly.

As you stake the layout, remember that no part of your fence, including the concrete footings, should cross property lines unless you have a written agreement with your neighbors (to avoid future disputes). As a matter of course, fence builders often stake out the fence line so that it falls at least 6 inches inside the legal boundaries, just to be on the safe side.

During the layout stage, your string lines indicate the exact centerline of the fence (along its length). Later, when you're setting and aligning the posts, you will reposition the string lines to indicate the outside surface of the fence. But for now, you want to make sure they are exactly where you want them to be—each section forming the angle you want with the adjacent one. To stake your fence-line layout, follow the steps below.

Tools and Supplies

Look over the illustration and text to familiarize yourself with the basic procedures. Then use this list to make sure you have the tools and supplies you'll need.

- Mason's twine (it doesn't break when stretched taut)
- Stakes and 1 by 3s for batter boards
- Box nails
- Hammer
- Sledge hammer
- Measuring tape (50 or 100 feet)
- Framing square

The Steps of Layout

1. Install the batter boards. Drive a pair of stakes (about 18 inches apart) securely into the earth 2 to 4 feet beyond the end point of each section of fence line. (Use your fence-line layout plan as a reference. See page 54). If the fence will abut an existing house wall or fence, drive the stakes in just in front of it.

2. Nail a length of 1 by 3 across the outside faces of the stakes, using two nails per stake. See the detail of a batter board below.

3. Stretch a string line between each pair of batter boards. Make sure it's taut, as this is the only way it can indicate a perfectly straight line. If the distance between batter boards is so long that the string won't stay taut, add a third batter board at midspan and tie a separate line well taut between each pair.

If bushes or other obstructions impinge on the line, you won't get the accurate reading you need. If the impingement can be removed, propped out of the way, or trimmed back, do that. If it's a permanent part of the landscape, such as a rock outcropping that the fence will have to go around, lengthen the batter-board stakes so that the string line clears it.

Where level earth begins to slope, establish a batter board at the break and continue the line from there. At these points you'll have to sight down the line from the top of the slope to be sure it hasn't inadvertently skewed off the centerline you've just established over level ground.

4. Adjust the string lines. Move the string lines along the batter boards to adjust their positions. Double-check to be sure that their placement reflects the positions you had in mind when you made the design. For instance, if a section of fence was planned to parallel a terrace or the wall of a house, measure from those existing site features to see if the line is properly placed. Adjust it accordingly. Where two sections of fence line abut, or where a section terminates against an existing wall, carefully check their intersection to make certain they're correctly angled to each other. For right angles, use the 3-4-5 triangle measuring technique illustrated below. (For other angles, a simple sight check will probably be enough.)

When everything is placed just as you'd like it to be, you're ready to mark out the posthole locations.

3-4-5 Triangle Measuring Technique

Measure and mark a point along one string line a distance of 3 feet (from the intersection) and a distance of 4 feet along the other. Then measure the distance between those two points. If it doesn't exactly equal 5 feet, adjust the string lines until it does. The angle is then a perfect 90 degrees. A framing square can also give you a quick check.

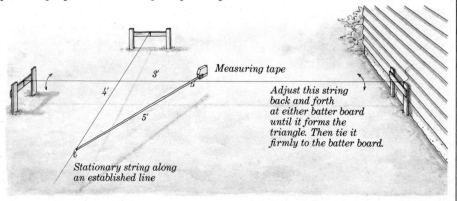

Measuring tape

Adjust this string back and forth at either batter board until it forms the triangle. Then tie it firmly to the batter board.

Stationary string along an established line

A Sample Fence Line Layout

This is the fence line layout for the sample site plan shown on pages 20-23. It is a side view of that plan.

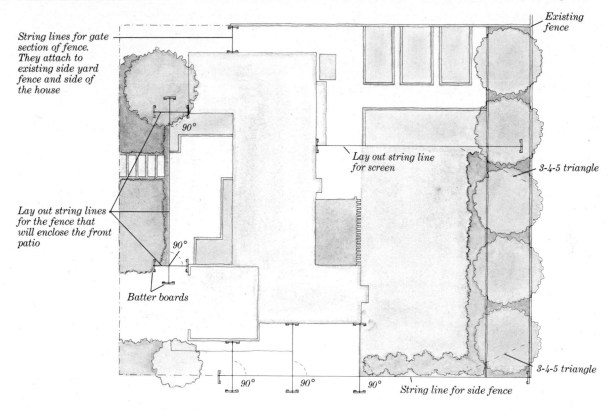

String lines for gate section of fence. They attach to existing side yard fence and side of the house

Existing fence

90°

Lay out string line for screen

3-4-5 triangle

Lay out string lines for the fence that will enclose the front patio

90°

Batter boards

90°   90°   90°

3-4-5 triangle

String line for side fence

Batter Board Detail

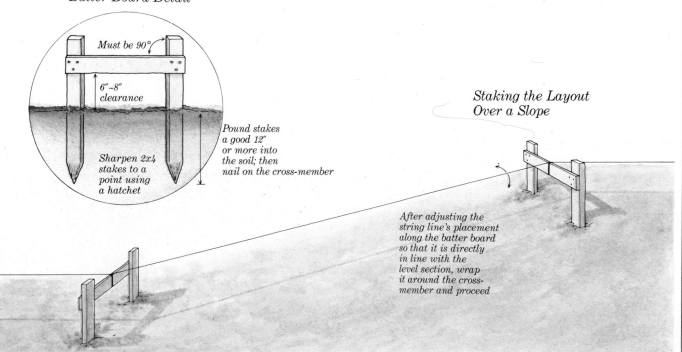

Must be 90°

6"–8" clearance

Sharpen 2x4 stakes to a point using a hatchet

Pound stakes a good 12" or more into the soil; then nail on the cross-member

Staking the Layout Over a Slope

After adjusting the string line's placement along the batter board so that it is directly in line with the level section, wrap it around the cross-member and proceed

Mark and Dig the Postholes

Mark the Postholes

Accurately marked posthole positions not only ensure a pleasing visual rhythm in the finished fence, they also make it a lot easier to build—minimizing the need to do special measuring and cutting to fit.

Marking posthole locations consists of two phases. First, measure and mark the string line where posts will be placed; then mark and flag those locations on the ground. Then dig the holes at the flagged locations.

Use the fence-line layout plan as a reference. Don't be discouraged if you have to adjust your plans a bit. As they take shape in three-dimensional form, things can change a little, sometimes even a lot. You may want to adjust the post spacing accordingly (see pages 54-55 for how to divide the fence line into bays).

You will need the following tools and supplies for marking the posthole locations:
- Measuring tape
- Plumb bob
- Masking tape
- Cloth scraps and long nails, or a can of spray paint, or flour or powdered chalk for flagging.

Here's the step-by-step procedure for marking, cutting, and digging postholes.

1. Check the post spacing. Before you assume that the post spacing you've planned on paper will divide up precisely in the field, it's a good idea to double-check. To do this, measure the overall length of each section of fence and compare the figures with those on your plan. Are they the same? If not, you'll need to adjust the fence line divisions (see pages 54-55 for three easy ways to deal with the problem).

2. Measure and mark the posthole locations. The locations are marked *on center,* from the center of one post to the center of the next. Since the string line indicates the linear center line of the fence, the exact center point of a corner post is where two string lines cross. This is a good place to start your measuring for marking the posthole locations.

When you've confirmed or adjusted the post spacing so that it works out, measure along the string line and mark each location by wrapping a little masking tape flag around the line.

3. Mark the posthole locations on the ground. When all the locations have been marked on the string line, use a plumb bob to mark them on the ground. Flag the spot by poking a nail through a scrap of cloth at the point of the plumb bob, by dropping a handful of flour or chalk there, or by giving the spot a spray of nontoxic paint.

When you've completed the job, leave the batter boards in place; you will soon use them to reestablish the string lines in a new position to guide you in setting and aligning the posts. Cut a little V-notch in the batter board where the string line now rests (or mark it with an indelible pen) so you can find the right position later.

Then untie the lines so that you have open access for digging the postholes.

Flagging Posthole Locations

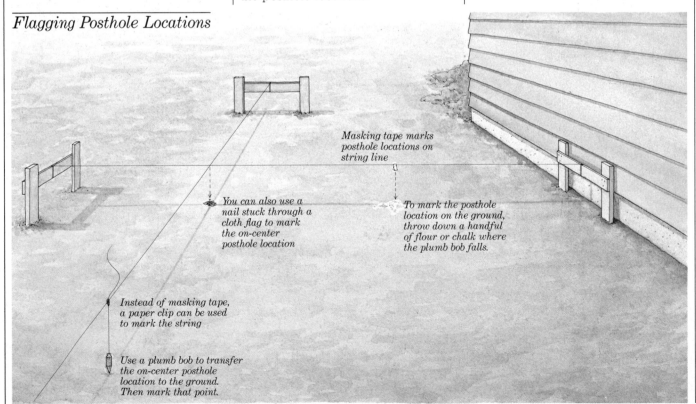

Masking tape marks posthole locations on string line

You can also use a nail stuck through a cloth flag to mark the on-center posthole location

To mark the posthole location on the ground, throw down a handful of flour or chalk where the plumb bob falls.

Instead of masking tape, a paper clip can be used to mark the string

Use a plumb bob to transfer the on-center posthole location to the ground. Then mark that point.

Marking a Slope

You'll use a different technique to mark posthole locations on a slope so that posts will be evenly spaced according to the run of the slope. (If you measure along the actual grade, they will be closer together than the posts on level ground.)

To do this, you'll need to make up a layout stick. Cut a 1 by 4 equal to the on-center size of the bay. Then drive a tall stake into the earth so that its surface is precisely flush with the last posthole flag. With the aid of a helper, as shown below, butt the layout stick to the stake and move it up or down the stake until the mark at the other end intersects the string and the layout stick is level. Flag the point and repeat the process. Take the stake with you and pound it in at each new position.

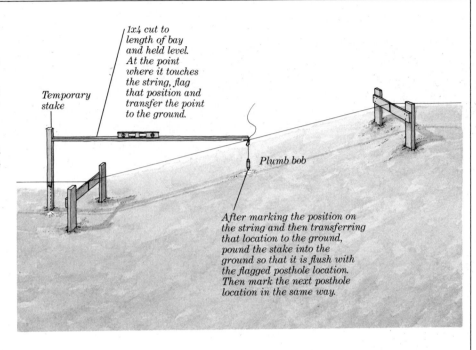

Temporary stake

1x4 cut to length of bay and held level. At the point where it touches the string, flag that position and transfer the point to the ground.

Plumb bob

After marking the position on the string and then transferring that location to the ground, pound the stake into the ground so that it is flush with the flagged posthole location. Then mark the next posthole location in the same way.

Dig the Postholes

Digging postholes is hard work. The more you dig in a day, the more resoundingly this truth comes home. To make the job as easy as possible, choose the proper posthole digging tool for the situation at hand.

Tools

How many holes do you need to dig? If there are more than about a dozen, consider using a power-driven earth auger, or hire a drilling firm to do the job. If you have only a few holes to dig, a hand tool will work just fine. In either case, posthole digging tools can be rented at tool rental outlets, lumberyards, or hardware stores.

If you plan to use a power auger, choose a tool that will give you the proper diameter hole for your post size. One-person augers have a smaller bit than two-person augers.

If you plan to dig the holes by hand, don't even consider using a shovel. It can't give you the clean, straight-sided hole needed to stabilize the fence posts. For rocky soil, a clamshell digger works better than an earth drill, though the double han-

dles tend to break down the sides of the hole if you need to dig them much beyond 2 feet deep, and a steel digging bar is practically essential to loosen the soil.

If the soil is loose and free of rocks, a single-handled earth drill or a bladed scoop digger will work well.

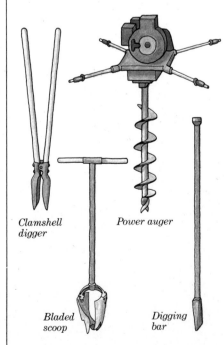

Clamshell digger

Power auger

Bladed scoop

Digging bar

Review the chart on page 60 to see how wide and how deep each post should be. (Terminal posts—end, corner, and gate posts—are typically larger than line posts and are set deeper.)

Technique

There is no special technique for digging postholes, though the aim is to cut a plumb hole to sufficient depth with clean, straight sides. If you can undercut the hole (make it wider at the base than at the top), all the better; this is the best way to anchor the post in the earth.

Once all the holes are dug, clean out the bottoms so that no loose earth remains. If you're using concrete post footings, clean up the diggings; spread them evenly in surrounding planting beds or cart them away. If you're using earth-and-gravel backfill footings, keep the soil for the mix.

Then shovel about 6 inches of gravel into the bottom of each hole for drainage. A rock in the bottom of each hole makes a solid post foundation. (If you have some rocks on site, put one in the bottom of each hole and then add enough gravel to create the 6-inch drainbed.)

Set the Posts

Setting the posts is the most important part of your fence installation. If they are plumb and in perfect alignment, you'll breeze through the rest of the construction process. The fence will be upright, handsome, straight, and true. If they aren't plumb or are poorly aligned, it means a lot of extra fitting and special cutting to coax the parts together in a sound and attractive way.

If your fence style uses dado or mortise joints to house the stringers in the posts, you'll need to set the posts to the exact height (see the box on the next page for instructions). Otherwise, you don't have to be so careful about the height of the posts, since you will cut the entire line of posts to the proper height later.

Setting the posts consists of five phases, all of which are much easier if you don't have to do them alone.

1. Restretch the string lines between the batter boards so they now indicate the outside surface of the fence posts. Measure the actual thickness of the end post (remember, for instance, that a 6 by 6 doesn't measure a full 6 inches) and divide that measurement by 2. Retie the string line that distance away from the V-notch on the batter board, moving it toward the outside of the fence.

2. For each section of fence, place, plumb, and brace the end posts in their holes. Stand an end post in the hole and twist its base into the gravel bed about 2 inches. Add a couple of braces (1-by-3 or 1-by-4 boards) about two-thirds of the way up the post on two adjacent faces. These

need to pivot, so use only one nail per brace (a duplex nail is easy to remove later). Then, with the aid of your helper, plumb the post on two adjacent faces with a 2-foot level. One person holds the post in position while the other aligns and plumbs it. When everything is just right, pound a stake firmly into the earth next to the bottom of each brace, and use a couple of box nails to fasten the brace to the stake. Repeat the process for the other end post.

3. Place, align, and brace the line posts. When both end posts are aligned and braced, stretch another string line between them about 18 inches below the top of the posts on the same face as the first string line.

Aligning and Bracing Posts

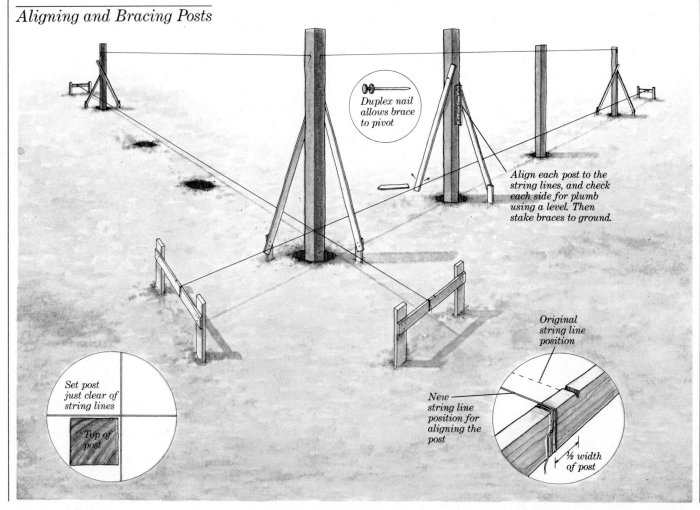

Duplex nail allows brace to pivot

Align each post to the string lines, and check each side for plumb using a level. Then stake braces to ground.

Set post just clear of string lines

Top of post

Original string line position

New string line position for aligning the post

½ width of post

Now proceed down the line, placing, aligning, and bracing each successive line post, just the way you did for the end posts. The string lines will help you position them accurately, but don't let the posts touch the strings. Line posts are smaller than end posts, so the string can indicate when the post is aligned, but if the post were to touch the string, it wouldn't be centered in the hole.

4. When all the posts are braced, set them permanently in their footings (see illustrations) one by one down the line. Double-check each post for alignment and plumb.

Earth-and-Gravel Footings

The key to making the posts fully secure in this type of footing is to tamp each successive layer of backfill vigorously once it's placed in the hole. The best tool to use for tamping is the shovel handle. It fits easily in the hole, punches the backfill down tight, and the weight of the shovel blade adds extra heft to each tamping stroke. You can use the end of a 2 by 2 or a 2 by 4 if that's easier for you to manage. Overfill the hole so that you can cap it with a slope from post to earth. This helps the footing

shed water rather than having it collect around the post where it will promote rotting. You can strip the braces from the posts when you've finished setting the footing; but if they don't obstruct the mounting positions of the stringers, take advantage of the extra strength by leaving them in place while completing the frame.

Concrete Post Footings

Whether you mix your concrete from scratch (1 part cement to 3 parts sand and 5 parts gravel) or from premixed sacks, the batch should be stiff and able to pack into a ball in your hand. You will have about 20 minutes before the mix begins to set up and get rigid. Make sure the bottom 2 inches of post are embedded in gravel before placing concrete in the hole. Then, by shovelful, place the concrete in the hole; poke it with a pipe or a broomstick to work out any air pockets. Overfill the hole at the top and crown off the concrete (slope it) using a mortar knife, to keep water from collecting around the post.

Leave the braces in place until the concrete has set up and cured. If they aren't in your way, you can leave the braces in place even as you add the stringers for extra support.

Setting a Post in Gravel

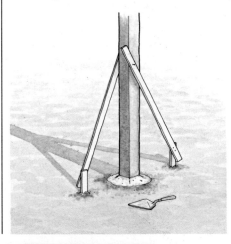

Setting a Post in Concrete

Setting Mortised or Dadoed Posts

Since mortise or dado joints predetermine the stringer positions, posts for these types of fences must be precisely set to height. Figure out how much post you want to have above the ground, then measure down that distance from the top of the end post. Fasten a pair of cleats at that point (as shown here), and position the post in its hole. Plumb, align, and brace it; then repeat for the other end post.

Stretch a string line over the tops of the posts and adjust them until the string is level. Then set the remaining posts, using this string line to gauge the proper finished height.

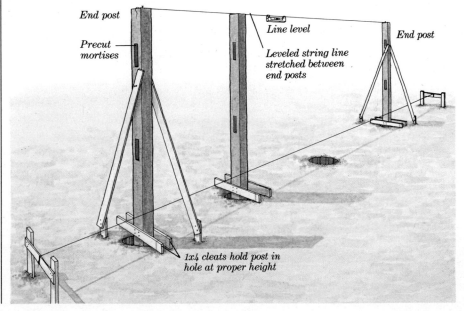

End post

Precut mortises

Line level

Leveled string line stretched between end posts

End post

1x4 cleats hold post in hole at proper height

Cut the Posts and Add Stringers

If you set the posts at random heights, now is the time to cut them to length. This procedure is done in three phases.

First, you'll snap chalk lines on the line of posts to mark the placement positions for the stringers.

Second, you'll install the top stringers—marking, cutting to length, and nailing them in place—one by one until all have been installed.

Third, you'll install all the bottom stringers, using the same techniques.

So now it's time to put on your nail belt and fill the pouches. A generous use of nails is the secret to a fence's longevity and appearance, especially at this stage. Follow the instructions and illustrations below. See the box for nailing patterns and techniques.

1. Measure and mark the posts for cutting height. On your elevation sketch, see how tall the posts (not the infill) should be. From the ground, measure up the post to the proper height and mark that point on the yard-side face of one end post. Fasten a nail at that point and secure a chalk line to it. Run the chalk line out to the other end post.

If the fence is on level ground, use a string level to level the chalk line; pull it taut and snap it.

If the fence is on a slope, measure up the end post to the proper height and snap the chalk line there. Make sure all posts are marked; you may need to resnap the line.

2. Mark each post with cutoff guidelines. For posts in level ground, and for posts that will form stepped frames, use a try square to carry the chalk-line marks around the post. (For stepped frames, the chalk line will be angled on the face of the post. Use the lower end of the line as your marking point and carry it around square; ignore the higher end.)

For posts that will form stepped frames, you will simply cut the post off at the indicated chalk-line angle. If you need guidelines on all four faces to help you make an accurate cut, just carry the lines around so that they indicate the cutting angle.

3. Use a handsaw or a hand-held power saw to cut each post to height. Use a ladder to be able to see your guidelines, and hold the tool in a safe and comfortable position.

4. Add the stringers. Distribute the stringers around the perimeter of the fence line so assembly can move more quickly. You can remove the braces if they are in your way, but if they're not, they'll give the developing frame some extra stability.

Carrying Marks

Chalk mark carried

Snapped chalk line

Saving the Line

Marked cut line

Saw just to the outside of the marked cutting line; that way the length of the board you marked is the length of board you get.

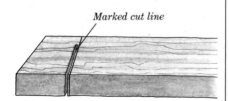

Marking Posts for Cutting

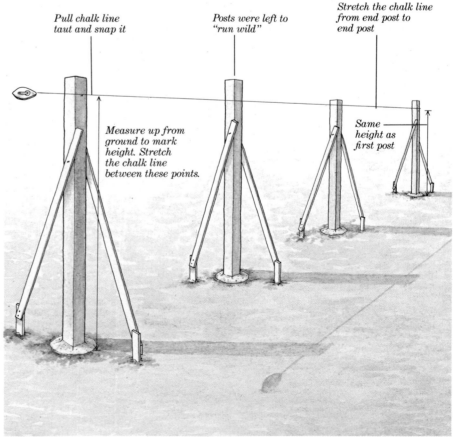

Pull chalk line taut and snap it

Posts were left to "run wild"

Stretch the chalk line from end post to end post

Measure up from ground to mark height. Stretch the chalk line between these points.

Same height as first post

Always measure the stringer positions from the top of the posts down. Measure the placement positions of the top and bottom stringers on each end post and fasten a nail at those points. Run a chalk line between those points and adjust it for level, or correct its angle. Then pull it taut and snap it.

For stepped frames or for sloped frames over uneven terrain, the stringer positions for each successive pair of posts will have to be measured and marked separately. For frames on level ground or on an even slope, you can mark an entire section of the fence line at once by snapping a continuous chalk line.

5. Mark and cut top stringers to length and nail them in place. There are two ways to mark the stringers to be cut to length: one is to use a measuring tape, and the other is to simply hold the stringer in position and mark it. Then cut it to length and nail it in place. If you use the second marking technique, the stringer should be held to the posts exactly where it will be mounted and in the proper position, either on-edge or on-flat. (Be sure when you cut the stringer to length that you ''save the line''—cutting just to the outside of your marks—so that you get a snug fit.) Work your way around the fence, marking, cutting, and nailing all the top stringers in place.

6. When the top of the frame is all tied together, go back and mark, cut to length, and nail the bottom stringers in place. When the frame is complete, strip away any bracing that remains and clean up the debris.

Set up to add the infill by distributing your materials around the perimeter of the fence line.

Installing the Stringers

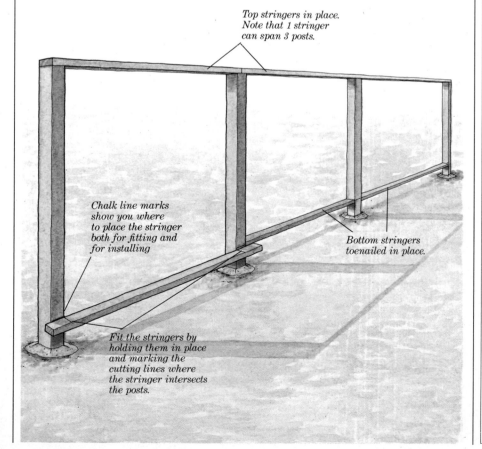

Top stringers in place. Note that 1 stringer can span 3 posts.

Chalk line marks show you where to place the stringer both for fitting and for installing

Bottom stringers toenailed in place.

Fit the stringers by holding them in place and marking the cutting lines where the stringer intersects the posts.

Nailing Techniques and Patterns

For stringers that overlay the posts, either on-flat or on-edge, use a four- or five-nail pattern as shown below. All are face-nailed.

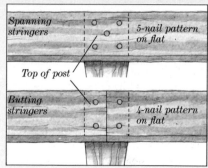

Spanning stringers · 5-nail pattern on flat · Top of post · Butting stringers · 4-nail pattern on flat

For stringers that butt between the posts, use a six-nail pattern. All the nails are toenailed.

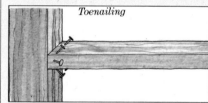

Toenailing

To make nailing easier, ''start'' your nails first, then position the stringer and hammer the nails all the way in.

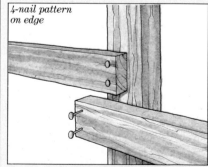

4-nail pattern on edge

If you find that the nails tend to split the lumber, blunt the point of the nail a bit before starting it.

Blunting nails

Add the Infill

You have now arrived at the best part of all; your idea takes shape in full and final form. Adding the infill seems like the fastest, easiest part of the installation, no matter how much or how little nailing it requires. After all, the end is in sight, and since the processes repeat, you can build up a good rhythm and speed and still work with skill.

Because there are so many styles of infill, and each one is treated a little differently, this section presents the subject in its two broadest categories: *nail-on* infill mountings and *inset* mountings. Most types of infill can be mounted either way, depending on the finished effect you want.

Look at both processes and see the tips, techniques, and guidelines illustrated and described on the following pages. Then it should be easy for you to follow the installation processes and techniques that apply to the style you have chosen.

Nail-On Infill

Nail-on fence styles are faster to build than inset fences; and depending on which face you see, the surface looks quite different—though both can be attractive. For this type of infill mounting over level earth, you don't need to precut the infill to length (unless the tops have a cut detail, as pickets and grape stakes do). You can let the board ends "run wild"—be random heights—at the top and cut them to a finished line in one fell swoop later.

Here's how to do it.

1. Distribute the infill materials around the perimeter of the fence line so that it's close at hand when you start to install it.

2. Nail tack strips or stretch string lines between posts to act as placement guides for the bottom edges of the board. (You can do this about three or four bays at a time and then move them up to the next series of bays when you get there.)

If the terrain is evenly sloped, guidelines here will help you; but if it is uneven and you're running the infill along the contour, just eyeball

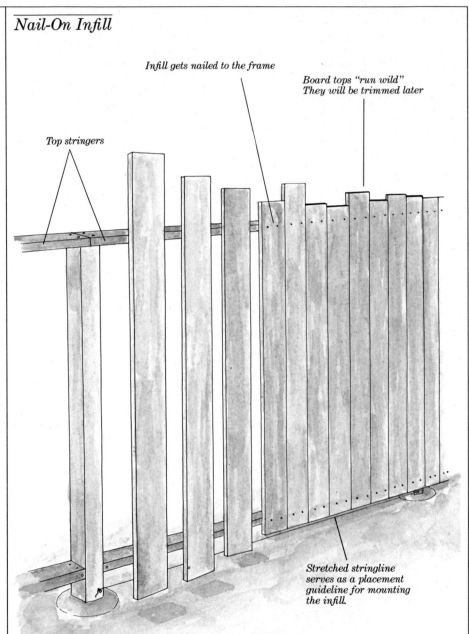

Nail-On Infill

Top stringers

Infill gets nailed to the frame

Board tops "run wild" They will be trimmed later

Stretched stringline serves as a placement guideline for mounting the infill.

the placement of the bottom edge of each successive board instead.

3. Begin mounting the infill at the end, corner, or gate post. Nail it up board by board until all the infill is fastened in place. Every 3 or 4 feet, use a level on the edge of the last board to make certain that the infill is plumb. If it gets out of plumb, correct the discrepancy by adjusting the placement of the next few boards.

4. When you've finished, measure and mark the cutoff line along the top edge of the fence at the end of each section. Snap chalk lines between those points. If you use a hand-saw, that will be the cutoff line. If you use a hand-held power saw, measure down from the chalk line a distance equal to the blade's offset from the edge of the saw's shoe. (See the following page for an illustrated example of this process.)

Inset Infill

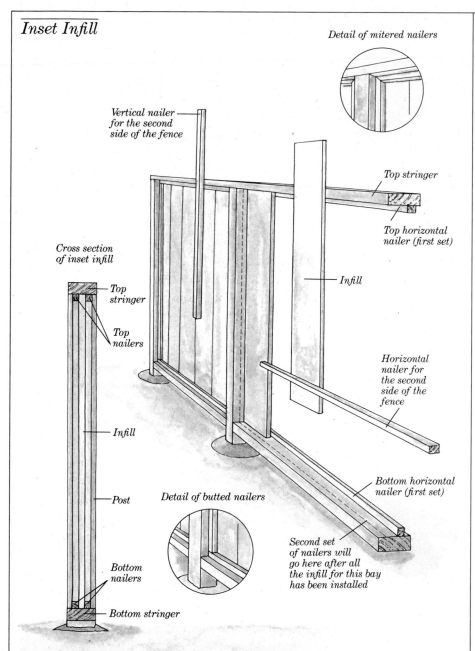

Detail of mitered nailers

Vertical nailer for the second side of the fence

Top stringer

Top horizontal nailer (first set)

Infill

Cross section of inset infill

Top stringer

Top nailers

Infill

Post

Bottom nailers

Bottom stringer

Detail of butted nailers

Horizontal nailer for the second side of the fence

Bottom horizontal nailer (first set)

Second set of nailers will go here after all the infill for this bay has been installed

5. Tack on a cutting guide strip (1 by 3s, for example). Make sure the joints between them are even so that the saw's shoe doesn't catch at the joint and make a jog in the clean, finished top line you cut.

6. Cut the fence line to height and clear the yard of debris.

7. If you plan to finish the fence with a stain or paint, prepare surfaces according to the manufacturer's instructions. To protect your land-caping, cover surrounding plantings and earth with plastic tarps. When all is said and done, stand back and admire your work! You've created something very special.

Inset Infill

Fences with an inset infill require more careful construction than nail-on styles do, but they return a special beauty for the effort. Inset fences look clean-lined and gracefully refined, and they show an equally attractive face on both sides. The infill material can be precut to size, as long as you are quite sure the opening is in square and of a standard size.

1. Measure the height and width of the opening for several bays, or all of them if you think there might be discrepancies in size or squareness.

2. Check for squareness by holding a framing square in the corners of each bay, or measure the diagonals (if they're equal, the opening is perfectly square). If the opening isn't square, it won't show if board placements receive extra care; just let them absorb the discrepancy equally through the bay. (Rigid sheet materials can be cut to fit exactly.)

3. Precut the infill materials to length, both boards and nailing strips. Note that you can miter the strips for a special visual effect, or you can butt them; in the latter case, let the crosswise pieces extend the full width of the opening. The upright pieces will fit snugly between.

4. Measure and mark the nailing strip positions at a few points on each side of the frame. (You'll install the set of strips toward the outside of the fence first. This will give the boards a surface to rest against as you nail the infill in place.) Use box or finish nails to fasten the strips to the frame.

5. Toenail the infill boards to the frame, not the nailers, working from one side of the opening to the other. Occasionally check the edge of a board for plumb with a level. Correct any discrepancies by adjusting the placement of the next few boards.

6. Toenail the other set of nailers to the frame to cover the boards' unfinished edges. When you have completed all the bays, clean up the debris.

7. If you're planning a finish treatment, prepare surfaces according to the manufacturer's instructions. (Protect landscaping with plastic tarps.)

When all has come to an end, have a long look. The fence is bound to be a beauty.

Techniques for Installing Infill

The tips, techniques, and guidelines on these pages will make the job of installing infill faster and easier, and the fence will look better for it. There are several things to aim for when you install the infill. To make sure the infill is well fastened to the frame and is able to resist loads such as wind, weather, and general wear and tear, use plenty of nails or fasteners.

To keep boards plumb, check the infill every few feet with a 2-foot level. If the infill has gotten out of plumb, correct it by leaving small compensatory gaps between pieces until the discrepancy is corrected.

To keep spaces between pieces of infill even and regular, make a spacer. It will save you from measuring for each piece of infill. The cleat hangs in on the top stringer, freeing your hands to hold the infill in place as you nail.

To keep angled infill even, use a bevel square or make a template to properly position the infill to the frame.

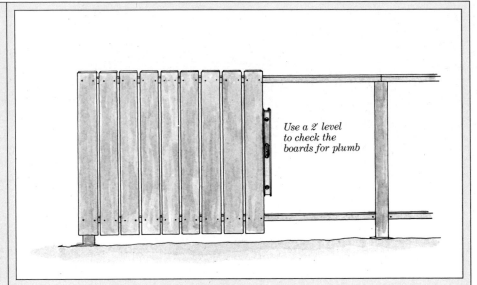

Use a 2' level to check the boards for plumb

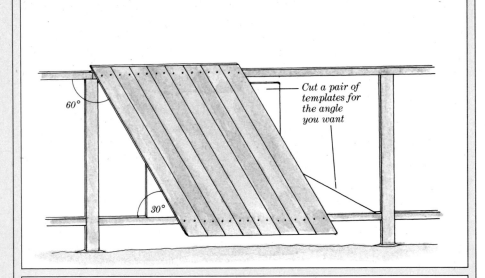

60°

30°

Cut a pair of templates for the angle you want

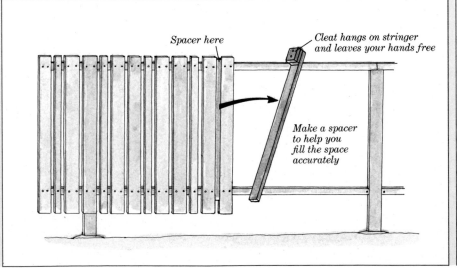

Spacer here

Cleat hangs on stringer and leaves your hands free

Make a spacer to help you fill the space accurately

To keep bottom edges flush and smooth, use guidelines to help you gauge your placement at a glance—unless your design intentionally calls for a random effect. You can stretch string lines between posts to guide you. Or tack a 1 by 3 or 1 by 4 to the surface of the posts, so that the infill has something to rest on while you nail it in place. Reposition the tack strips every few bays as you work your way down the line.

To finish a top edge that was left to run wild, measure and mark the cut-off line using a chalk line. Then lightly tack on a series of 1-by-3 or 1-by-4 cutting guides at a distance below the chalk line equal to the distance from the saw's blade to its shoe. Set the blade to a depth sufficient to cut through the infill, but no deeper. Rest the saw on the cutting guide and cut the entire top of the fence off in one pass.

To install kickboards, overlay them on the posts or inset them to the underside of the bottom stringer and attach to a nailer. Use pressure-treated lumber, or all-heart of a decay-resistant species, since the board touches the earth and is thus subject to rot. Kickboards are used to close the gap at the bottom (for visual purposes, to give a more finished look; or for functional ones, to keep animals from going under the fence).

To finish your fence, see pages 57 and 61.

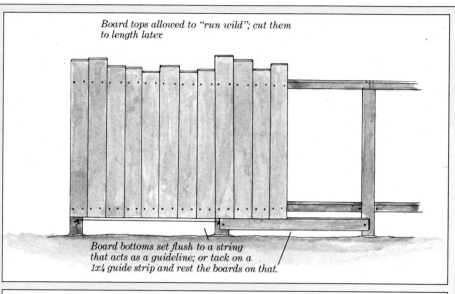

Board tops allowed to "run wild"; cut them to length later.

Board bottoms set flush to a string that acts as a guideline; or tack on a 1x4 guide strip and rest the boards on that.

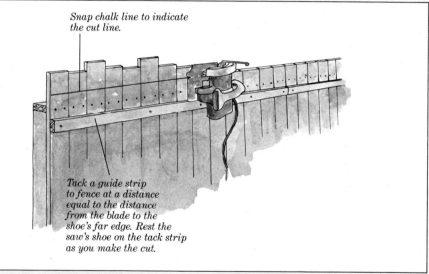

Snap chalk line to indicate the cut line.

Tack a guide strip to fence at a distance equal to the distance from the blade to the shoe's far edge. Rest the saw's shoe on the tack strip as you make the cut.

Post

Stringer

2x4 kickboard

Trim to fit concrete

Nailer fastened to stringer

Stringer

Kickboard fastened to nailer

Adding to an Existing Fence

It's easy to add new sections of fencing to an existing fence; simply determine the sizes of the parts—posts, stringers, and infill—and build the new to match the old.

The only crucial point is the one at which the new fence meets the existing one. The better they're fastened together, the more they'll work in tandem to bear the shared loads.

New sections of fencing will look best if you duplicate the wood species and finish of the existing fence. If the fence has weathered, the new sections will stand out until the weathering process catches up. But you can diminish the brand-new look by using quick-weathering techniques

and finishes. For example, on some species of wood, the application of stains or other chemical mixtures can weather it almost instantly. Choose a stain that matches the weathered tone of your existing fence. By the time the stain wears off, the fence will have weathered sufficiently underneath it to make it harmonize with the old.

Planning the Layout
The construction processes are the same ones used to build new fencing. First, take field measurements and plan the extent of the new section.

If you want to experiment with different layout options, you might want to make a rough sketch of the area you're considering (see pages

20-21). Then, to design the fence, measure the sizes of the existing fence members, the post locations, and the relationships of all the parts—stringer positions, special details, and so forth.

Materials
To determine how much of each type of material you'll need, make a sketch of what the fence will look like (one bay will be enough) and then compute the number of lineal feet of material you'll need for each fence part for that one bay. List it out and multiply them to figure the totals you'll need to complete the entire new section.

Extending an Existing Fence

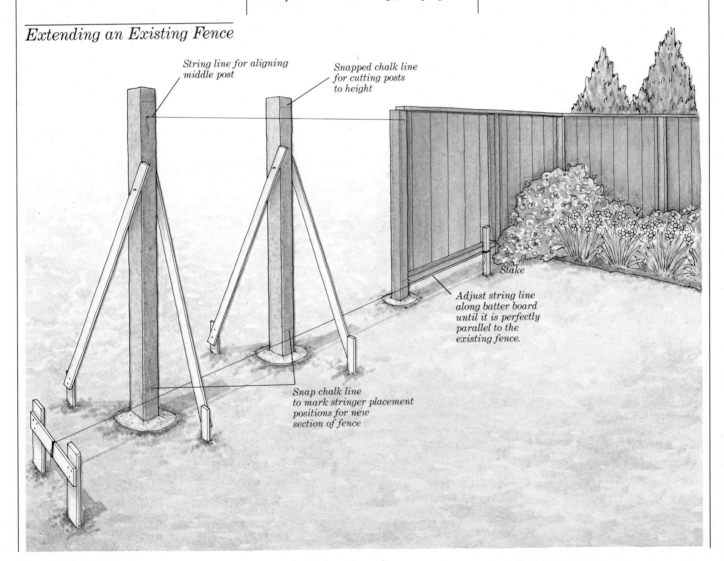

String line for aligning middle post

Snapped chalk line for cutting posts to height

Stake

Adjust string line along batter board until it is perfectly parallel to the existing fence.

Snap chalk line to mark stringer placement positions for new section of fence

Installing the Fence

To install the fence, first stake the layout. If the new section is to extend the length of an existing fence line, you will use a different kind of layout technique than that used for perpendicular fence-line additions.

Extending an Existing Fence Line

Pound a stake into the ground about 6 feet before the end of the old fence and about 1 inch away from it. Pound a batter board into the earth about 4 feet beyond the length of the new section. Tie a string line between these points, adjusting it along the batter board until it is an even 1 inch from the existing fence and exactly parallel to it. Measure and mark the posthole locations on the string and then on the ground; then flag them.

Adding a Perpendicular Section

Start the new section at an existing post. There, you can fasten the new stringers for the first bay directly into it. If this conflicts with your design, plan to add a new post; you'll also need to add a *mullion* (a midbay upright) between the existing stringers so that you have a good fastening surface for it.

Pound a batter board into the ground about 4 feet beyond the end of the new section. Stretch a string line from the existing fence to the batter board and square it up using the 3-4-5 measuring triangle (see pages 62-63). Measure out and mark your new post locations on the string line and then on the ground (see pages 64-65).

Dig the postholes, set the posts, and add the stringers and infill just as you would do for new fencing (see pages 64-73). If your fence section includes a gate opening, remember that gate posts should be larger than line posts and should be set deeper in the earth (see pages 52-53).

Installing a Perpendicular Addition

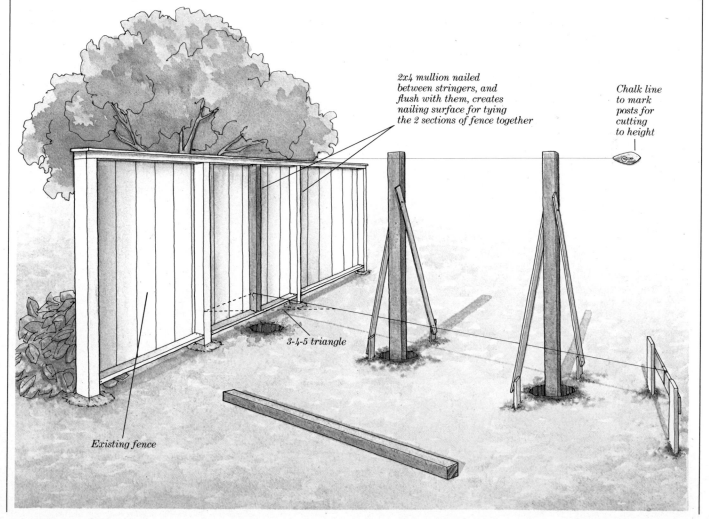

2x4 mullion nailed between stringers, and flush with them, creates nailing surface for tying the 2 sections of fence together

Chalk line to mark posts for cutting to height

3-4-5 triangle

Existing fence

Mending Fences

Most structural deterioration begins with the posts—at grade or below it where the problem can't be seen. Posts not only bear the weight of the fencing but serve to keep the structure vertical and true by transferring wind, wear, and weather loads down to the ground. As posts become weakened or thrown out of alignment by environmental forces, they can't do their structural job properly. This can result in a skewed or tilting fence, stringers that pull away from the posts, and infill that splits or twists loose from the framework.

None of these problems will go away if left alone, so treat fence maintenance as preventive medicine. If you give the fence a checkup in the spring or fall, while the ground is loose but not muddy, you'll probably be able to extend its life.

A Fence Post Checkup

Posts can lose their structural strength in more than one way: they can rot out; their footing can crack, loosen, or deteriorate; or they can simply give out due to improper alignment when the fence was built.

Check the Posts for Rot

For concrete footings, use an ice pick or other sharp tool to poke around the base of the post. For earth-and-gravel backfill, dig down about 6 inches around the base of the post to check for rot. In either case, if the wood is soft or spongy, rot has set in and the post will need to be replaced before it further weakens the fence.

Check for Plumb

If the posts aren't plumb, the fence won't be. If posts begin to tilt a little, the forces of nature will amplify that action, loosening and skewing them until the stringers eventually pull away from the posts and siding pulls free from the framework. To correct the problem, realign and reset the posts, refasten the stringers securely, and nail down the infill or siding. Vigorous plants working their shoots into existing fencing can also force joints apart. Cut them away from the fence and renail the joints.

Check the Surface Finish

Fences not only look better but wear better when the finish is able to repel decay-causing moisture. If yours is a painted or stained finish, recoating can add longevity to the fence. If the fence was left to weather naturally, a reapplication of water-repellent sealer won't change the color but it will help the fence shed water.

Repairing a Decayed Post

If the post was set with a concrete collar, use a wrecking bar to break up the concrete and remove it. If it was set with earth-and-gravel backfill, dig it out again.

1. Without detaching rails or siding, cut away the old post about 1 or 2 inches above ground level, or as close to that point as sound wood remains. Clean out the hole, taking care to keep the sides of it as straight as possible, to a depth of 30 inches.

If the fence is badly skewed or tilted, you can work it back upright bit by bit with the help of a *come-along* (a winchlike tool available at rental outlets).

2. Put 6 inches of gravel in the bottom of the hole. Cut a length of post (heartwood or pressure-treated material of the same dimensions as the original post) so that it will extend about 3 feet above the earth.

Mending Decayed Posts and Leaning Fences

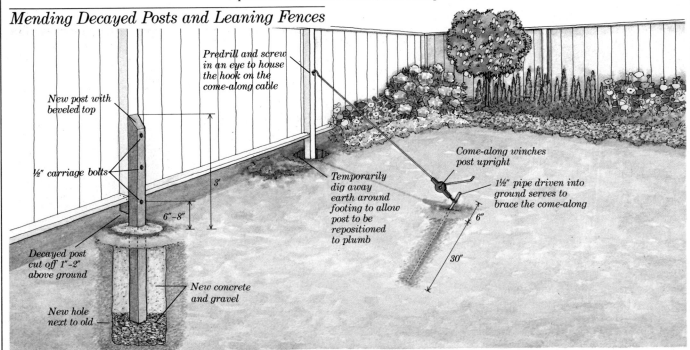

New post with beveled top

Predrill and screw in an eye to house the hook on the come-along cable

½" carriage bolts

Decayed post cut off 1"–2" above ground

6"–8"

3'

New hole next to old

New concrete and gravel

Temporarily dig away earth around footing to allow post to be repositioned to plumb

Come-along winches post upright

1½" pipe driven into ground serves to brace the come-along

6"

30"

Cut the top of it to a 45-degree angle so that it can shed water. You may have to saw off the most stubbornly leaning posts (at the base of the fence) to pull the fence into an upright position.

3. Place the post in the hole, work it several inches into the gravel bed, and mark bolt positions so that the lowest bolt is 6 to 8 inches above the earth—or above that if the wood isn't fully sound to that point.

4. Drill holes to accept ½-inch carriage bolts, and securely fasten the two sections of post together. If the fence needs plumbing, do so and brace it in place. Add concrete and crown the top. When the concrete has set (48 hours), remove the braces.

Repairing a Leaning Fence

If the fence is leaning or skewed along a section of its length, either because many posts have rotted out or because earth movement has forced the structure out of alignment, you may be able to add new midspan posts to reposition and support the existing fence.

1. Brace the fence with 2 by 4s so that it doesn't fall over. Then dig out the earth or break out the concrete collars around the errant posts so that you can set the fence back upright. Don't remove any stringers or infill. These are key parts of the fundamental structural strength of the existing fence, and you want to keep that intact as much as possible.

2. To pull the fence back into alignment, work in stages. Pull the fence a little at the end posts, then at the next posts, then the next, and back again, bracing each amount of gain you achieve. To do this, use a pulley or a come-along. Both are available at tool rental outlets.

3. When the fencing is upright and braced in a plumb position, determine the on-center position for the new midspan posts. The repair will be most unnoticeable if you put the new posts at the exact center of each existing bay.

4. Measure and mark posthole locations. When you have the postholes marked, dig them out with a clamshell digger. Place the holes so that the new posts will be centered in the holes and notched in to stand flush with the existing framework.

5. Shovel 6 inches of gravel into the bottom of each hole. Place the post in the hole and work it about 2 inches into the gravel bed. Plumb it and mark the notching positions on both the stringer and the post. (Each will receive half of the other to make a tight, flush joint.)

6. Notch both the new midspan post and the existing stringer, and nail the new post securely in place. Check for plumb, and adjust the bracing as needed.

7. When all posts are braced and nailed, fill the postholes with concrete and crown the footings with a slope so that they shed water.

8. When the concrete is fully set (48 hours), remove the bracing and renail any loose stringers or infill that may have worked free. Don't use the same nail holes. If the wood is dry, it may split as you nail, so drill pilot holes first, using a drill bit slightly smaller than the nail's shank.

9. At the base of the fence, saw off and remove the remains of any deteriorated posts and refill the holes with the dirt from the new ones. Restain the new posts or give them a quick-weathering treatment to make the repair less noticeable.

Adding a Post Mid-Span

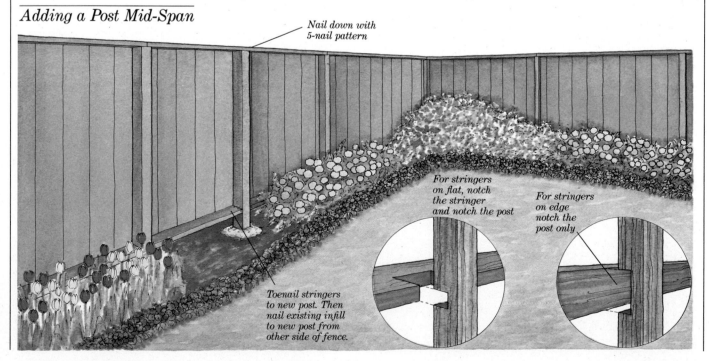

Nail down with 5-nail pattern

For stringers on flat, notch the stringer and notch the post

For stringers on edge notch the post only

Toenail stringers to new post. Then nail existing infill to new post from other side of fence.

GATES

There's something magical about a gate... each one seems to have a unique character, some special quality about it that people recognize, come to know, and enjoy. It's impossible to say how or why something as simple as a gate can become a memorable acquaintance... just what it is about a gate that engenders such affection.

Perhaps it's because gates are active players in an otherwise passive plane of the fence. Even an infrequently used or purely utilitarian gate—one that gives access to a service yard once a day or a couple of times a week—performs a valuable role in the scheme of things.

Or perhaps gates grow memorable because they render a double service—to separate as well as to join. They create a boundary, but at the same time will open to join person and place together again.

And maybe it's because gates and gateways promise an experience—a transition from that place to this one, a shift from then to now, leaving behind what was, stepping into what is and will be. There's a tiny, marvelous magic in that, and every gateway gives it. Even those that have grown rickety (having carried one too many children astride) and that now sag or squeak or drag grow more precious for their service. They're endured, treated gently, carefully repaired, and renewed. It's no wonder, then, that gates win an appreciation. There's something friendly about a gate, something pleasant to see, to approach, and to pass through—if only once, or again and again.

That tiny, magic moment of leaving the past behind to join what is to be seems to capture the nature of the gate. This old rail gate might have creaked open to share a thousand slumbering afternoons.

WHAT KIND OF GATE?

The gate; the bound-
ary break; the place
where two worlds
join, where outside goes
in, where inside reaches
out—special places where
exclusion gives way to access, entry, invitation, and
welcome.

Gates can be designed to be a
focal point, punctuating the entry or
highlighting some special area on
site. Or they can be discreet, con-
cealing their purpose by appearing
to be only a continuation of the fence.
They can mirror the lines of the fence
and yet counterpoint the style by
using similar materials in a different
way. Or the gate can be made in an
entirely different material and by
contrast become a featured architectural element in its own right.

There's a lot you can do with a
gate, and it, in turn can do a lot for
you. It can create an image, project
an impression, and signal with a silent
language how you would like others
to approach. A tall, solid, locked gate
gives no permission to enter, save to
those who hold the key. But a little
painted picket gate that spans a path
with modest charm lets those who
approach know that it is ready and
willing to welcome them in. Some
gates stand open, ceremonious, and
on reserve—others, sentrylike, on
guard, signaling "state your business" to those who pass through.
Some are strictly utilitarian; others are
whimsically fantastic and free.

And then there are those that are
arbored or canopied, that extend you
a protected welcome with fanfare and
verve. Each one gives a message and
reflects something of the nature of the
place. There are many ways to design
your gate so that the spirit and impression it projects is the one you
want it to give.

Above: Situated at the top of
a rise of steps, this little gate,
nestled between cascades of
ferns and flowers, veils the
path beyond it with
an air of enchantment.
What lies beyond?

Above right: This gateway
seems to celebrate the play of
line, rhythm, and form. Bold,
simple shapes, massive scale,
and high color contrast are
bridged by a splashing
spray of green.

Below right: Contrast is the
keynote in this gateway.
Ornamental iron gates—
nicely proportioned and
specially crafted—provide a
rich contrast to the
world within.

WHAT KIND OF GATE?

Depending on their purpose and the impression you'd like them to give, some gates warrant more visual importance than others. A main-entry gate, for instance, might deserve a more prominent design than a gate that leads into a service yard. A gate can draw a lot of attention to itself or none at all, depending on its design and the type of material it's made of.

A gate can completely contrast with a fence. Metal gates, and wooden gates of a different style, announce their presence like an actor on center stage. By design, this gate treatment interrupts the fence line's visual continuity to highlight its place in the scheme of things.

A gate can exactly match a fence. Those that do, detail for detail, effectively conceal the fact of their existence. When you want to downplay the gate, a hinged one, mounted flush with the fence surface, will create a discreet effect.

A gate can also harmonize with the fence in style, but have distinguishing special effects, such as an openwork top or a particular trim detail. This invites attention to the gate without detracting from the visual continuity of the fence line.

In planning and designing your gate, the first step is to choose the type of material you'd like it to be made of—wood or metal. Wooden gates in a wood fence are a naturally pleasing combination, whether you buy a prefabricated gate or design one yourself. Metal gates in an ornamental iron fence are an enduringly attractive combination. However, metal gates in a wood fence need special consideration. They look best if used in counterpoint to an essentially solid-surfaced wood fence, classic and tailored, or a style that is simple, rectilinear, and clean-lined.

Metal gates can be custom designed and fabricated (see telephone directory listings under Ornamental Iron) or purchased prefabricated in stock sizes and styles. Appearance, quality, and price vary according to the gauge and type of metal and the size and design of the gate.

Above: The design and material of this great, wide wood gate stands in distinct contrast to its flanking stone wall. There's no question of where in the fence line the gateway is.

Below: Viewed from within, the only signal as to which section of fence doubles as a gate is the hardware, and even that is discreet. The gate exactly matches the fence, and its existence is concealed.

Right: The infill is the same for both fence and gate, but the gateway arches across the span, and the gate swoops down to mirror the curve, creating a vibrant kind of harmony.

Designing the Gate

For all its seeming simplicity—merely an operating section of fence—a gate is a fairly complex construction. Planning a gate requires careful thought, just as the building of it requires careful precision. Successful gates function smoothly and look good, even into old age, by taking advantage of the principle of teamwork.

Three "teams" are at work here: (1) *the gate:* adequate framing and bracing, appropriate joints, and well-fastened infill; (2) *the hardware:* hinges and screws or bolts, latches, catches, and locks, all sturdy enough to bear their load; (3) *the fence:* appropriately sized gate posts in suffi-

ciently deep holes, set with stable footings to transfer the load of the gate to the earth.

The task of the gate is to keep itself together, in square and flat. If the gate is too weak or too wide to structually support its own weight, the fence and hardware must bear the extra burden.

The hardware is pivotal. Its job is to connect the gate to the fence. Hardware that is asked to bear a heavier load than it is able will become overstressed, weaken, and lose its connecting grip.

The goal of the fence is to stay out of the way but provide support. Its job is to accept the load the hinges pass along and to transfer it down to the ground. To the extent that each part of the team does its own job well, the whole system is the better for it.

As you design the gate, keep in mind that the style of it—the infill and special details—are secondary issues. Any type of infill can be mounted on a frame to create the look you want. The primary design issues you need to address are structural ones. They must be solved in sequence, beginning with deciding how wide you want the gate or gates to be.

A Gate Is a Structural System

The style of the gate aside, its strength depends on its structural design, and its durability depends on how well it is built. In order for the gate to operate freely, it must be built in-square and be sturdy enough to stay that way. In addition, gates place a heavy load on adjacent sections of fence. To bear this load, gate posts are typically made of larger stock and set deeper than line posts. Finally, to join the parts of the system, you'll need to choose appropriately sized and designed operating hardware. See pages 90-91 for examples of latches, catches, hinges, and other gate accessories.

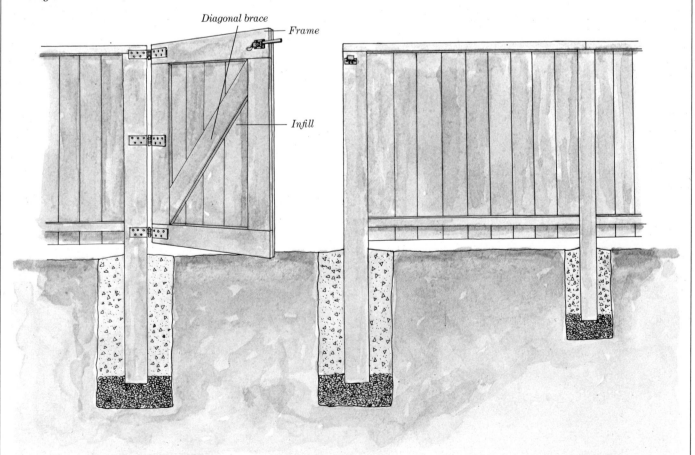

Diagonal brace

Frame

Infill

How Wide Is the Opening?

There are practical limits to the width of a gate before it's in danger of sagging out of square from the sheer load of its own weight. Tried-and-true tradition tells us that 4 feet is about the limit for a typically hinged, unsupported gate.

If your fence opening is wider than 4 feet, you have two options: you can either span the opening with a pair of gates or you can span it with one very wide gate that has extra supporting mechanisms—a supporting wheel, or a wire-and-turnbuckle assembly.

How Do You Want the Gate to Swing?

The illustrations here show you how the location of the gate, and the site conditions there, help you determine the direction in which the gate should swing. If you'd like it to swing in both directions, some types of hardware allow the gate to do this. See pages 90-91 for an overview of different kinds of gate hardware.

At the Edge of Your Property

Gates are typically mounted so they swing into your property rather than away from it. Under this condition, the gate should swing in one direction only.

Where One Fence Abuts Another

If it's convenient, gates are often mounted to hinge on the side of the fence that's nearest the corner so that views and access to livelier spots aren't inhibited by the swinging gate. Under this condition it can swing in one or both directions.

At the Top or Bottom of Stairs

If the landing is wider than the arc of the gate's swing, it's safe to mount a gate at the top or bottom of a flight of stairs. People need foot space in which to maneuver the gate, and the landing gives forewarning that steps exist beyond. Under these conditions the gate can swing in one or both directions.

Along a Slope

Gates are mounted to hinge on the low side of the slope so that as the gate swings open the bottom will clear the slope. Note that the frame is built in square, rather than conforming to the angle of the slope. Though it breaks the visual line of the fence framework, the gate gets the structural strength it needs. Under these conditions the gate can swing in one or both directions.

Across a Hillside

Gates are hung so they will swing out, toward the downhill direction, so that the bottom of the gate will swing free and clear of the slope of the hillside. Under these conditions it can swing in one direction only.

Designing the Gate

The choices and decisions that produce the design of your gate are easy to make, but there are many of them. So many, in fact, that getting them out of your head and down on paper will be a help in making a complete, clear plan before you begin to build.

Sketch the Gate Opening

Make a sketch to scale (1 inch equals 1 foot) of the gate opening and include several feet of fence on either side. Use this as the base drawing. To experiment with alternative design schemes, tape tracing-paper overlays on top of it. This will give you an accurate view of the visual effects for each choice you're considering. It's much easier to build the gate from a plan than it is to make it up as you go along, and the gate is much more likely to fit well and work freely.

Design the Details

Decide first whether you will close the opening with a single gate or a pair; whether the gate will match, harmonize, or contrast with the adjacent fence; and which direction it should swing. To help you decide those issues, sketch out the alternatives on graph paper.

When you have a clear picture of how you want the gate to look, choose the construction details: the framework that joins the parts of the gate into a single whole, and the hardware that makes it operate. In the illustrations here you see that there are two basic framework approaches: a Z-frame and a perimeter frame. Look them over and make a sketch or two to decide which one will work best for your gate. Some of these considerations can help you decide:

• The two types of frames are comparable in terms of serviceability, but a Z-frame is generally considered to have less structural strength than a perimeter frame.

• Both types of frames can take a nail-on infill, but only the perimeter

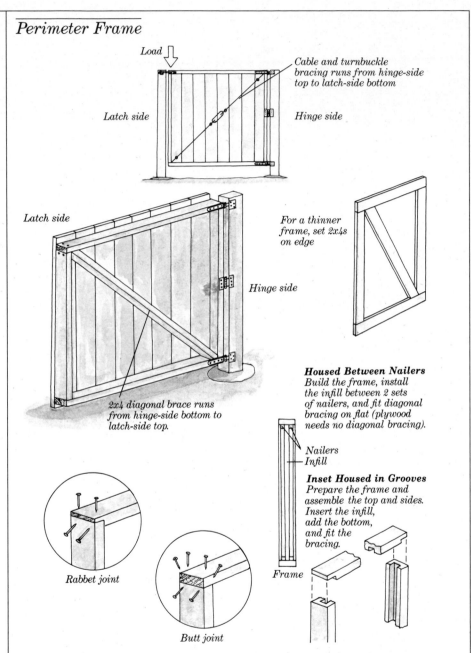

Perimeter Frame

Load

Cable and turnbuckle bracing runs from hinge-side top to latch-side bottom

Latch side

Hinge side

Latch side

Hinge side

For a thinner frame, set 2x4s on edge

2x4 diagonal brace runs from hinge-side bottom to latch-side top.

Housed Between Nailers
Build the frame, install the infill between 2 sets of nailers, and fit diagonal bracing on flat (plywood needs no diagonal bracing).

Nailers
Infill

Inset Housed in Grooves
Prepare the frame and assemble the top and sides. Insert the infill, add the bottom, and fit the bracing.

Frame

Rabbet joint

Butt joint

frame can house an inset infill, whether it's boards or a sheet material. (Prefabricated lattice panels, plywood, or plastic infill will look best mounted inset to a perimeter frame.)

• A Z-frame gives a light, casual look, in contrast to the perimeter frame, which tends to look a little more rectilinear and architectural.

After you have decided which type of frame will shape the gate, you're

ready to choose the construction details—the joints, stops, and hardware that will join it together.

First choose the joints to assemble the frame; they're shown above in accompaniment to the basic frames. Butt joints are the easiest to build, but they don't offer as much strength as rabbet joints or half-lap joints, which are a little harder to make.

Then choose a gate stop, which serves to save the hinges from need-

Z-Frame

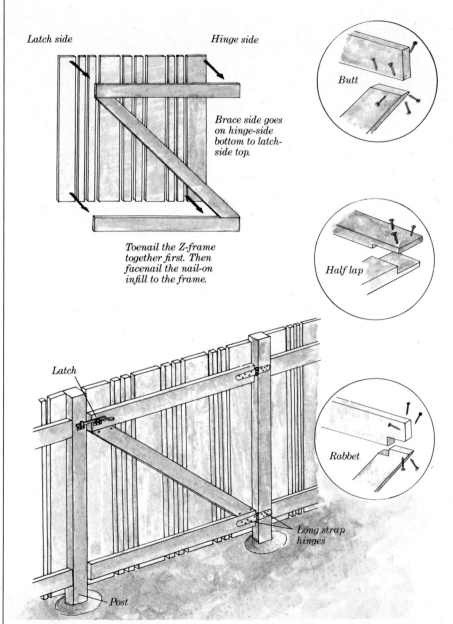

Latch side

Hinge side

Brace side goes on hinge-side bottom to latch-side top.

Toenail the Z-frame together first. Then facenail the nail-on infill to the frame.

Butt

Half lap

Rabbet

Latch

Long strap hinges

Post

The next two pages show you some ways to create a gate to go with a fence.

less overwork by giving the gate something to close against.

The next two pages show you some ways to create a gate to go with a fence. Note that the style of the fence can lend a pleasing theme for the gate—a starting point for designing a special character at any transition point. And then, on the two pages that follow, you'll see the basic hardware options. You might want to pre-

view these, too, since the hardware and the frame will work together, both structurally and aesthetically.

When you've made your choices for construction details (joints, gate stops, and hardware), and developed the design of the gate, sketch them into your plan. Then draw up a list of the materials you'll need to complete the gate.

Gate Stops

Gate stops can be made of wood as an integral part of the gate (see the four options in the box), or you can add a piece of hardware—a latch or catch—to stop the gate's closing swing.

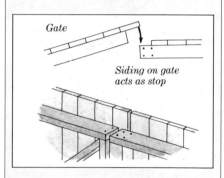

Gate

Siding on gate acts as stop

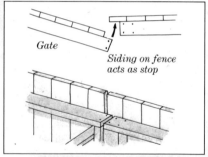

Gate

Siding on fence acts as stop

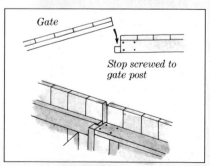

Gate

Stop screwed to gate post

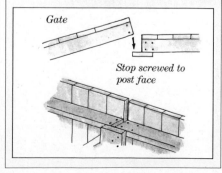

Gate

Stop screwed to post face

Designing the Gate

Gate Designs

The illustrations below show you examples of a variety of gate designs. If some major element in the fence—its materials, its color, or its pattern—are reflected in the gate, that will be enough to tie the look together into a unified whole. The gate designs shown here are influenced by the style of the fence, but they might also depart from it. Yours can, too.

Here, a simple plywood fence, elegantly toned in a classic color treatment, is dressed to the nines with an arched, glass gate. Bright brass hardware adds eye-catching sparkle and works perfectly well in the out-of-doors. Gate posts reach higher than the fence itself to support a lintel, announcing the special place a gateway is.

If your fence design sports some special detail, such as this openwork border cap, why not let the gate carry the theme and amplify the whole effect? The openings act like windows to the world beyond, but since they're placed high, the feeling of privacy on the inside isn't at all diminished, and you can't see into the area until you're close enough to the gate to open it.

A waist-high shingled wall with a contrasting colored cap offers such a pleasant boundary—neither understated nor overwhelming—that a matching gate only enhances the overall effect. Because the gate posts are the same color as the fence cap, the gate itself is clearly visible but remains discreet. And capping the gate to match the fence produces an attractive visual continuity as well.

Even a screen that suggests but does not enforce closure can be improved with the addition of a pair of gates to match. Paired gates are just as pleasant standing open, ready to invite passage freely, as they are functional when closed. Because this open fence design is scaled so large, the only real boundary it produces is a visual one, and gates for this type of screen primarily create continuity for that visual boundary.

Mixing materials is a nice way to call out a gate in a fence line, and metal gates give you a good opportunity to do that. Here, the gate design takes advantage of the fence style: The square metal "pickets" are set in a rhythm that mimics the pattern in the adjacent fence. The pickets of the gate remain the same, and the spaces between them differ in width, turning the pattern of the fence inside out.

Gate Hardware

If your eye has ever been caught by a strikingly handsome gate latch or a stunningly beautiful set of hinges, you know what a delightful design element the hardware on a gate can be. Beautifully designed, carefully fabricated gate hardware is special, and also seemingly rare. But it's not impossible to find.

The chart below gives you an overview of the commonly available types of gate hardware (hinges, latches, and catches) in a variety of styles.

If your building supply or hardware sources don't stock what you'd like to use, consider having some special hardware made at an ornamental iron shop, or even a brass foundry. Antique shops, salvage yards, and your own ingenuity at the work bench might also produce some interesting possibilities.

Clearances

Since required clearances between the gate and gate posts will vary, depending on the types of hardware you use, it's often recommended that you purchase your hardware before you begin to build the gate.

Hinges

No matter what type or style you select, remember that even lightweight gates are heavy and they're subject to the elements along with a tremendous amount of wear and tear. Three hinges hang a heavy gate far better than two can. Err on the side of excess when you select the hinges and fasteners—make heavy-duty and heavy-gauge your watchwords.

Screws

If the screws provided aren't long or strong enough to do the job they're asked to do, buy some that are. Screws should penetrate the wood frame as deeply as they can without coming through the other side.

Catches and Latches

Ring latch
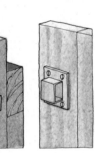

Top latch
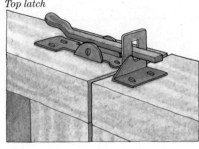

Slide bolt
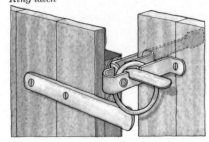

Slide action
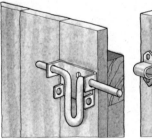

Hasp latch
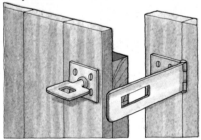

Strike latch
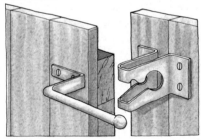

Thumb latch
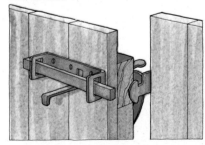

Lever latch
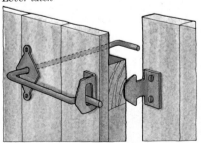

S latch

Loop latch
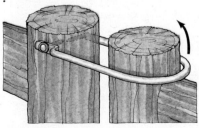

Hinges and Decorative Hardware

T-hinge

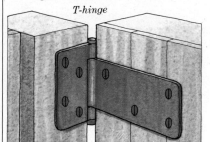

T-hinge

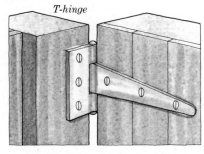

Strap hinge

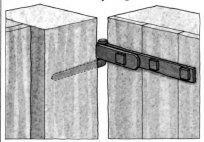

Butt hinge

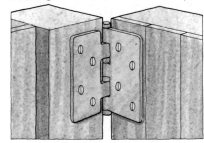

Screw hook and strap hinge

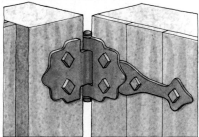

Screw hook and eye hinge

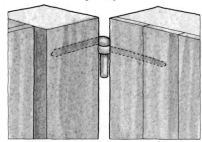

Ornamental T-hinge

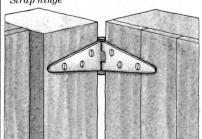

Strapped H-hinge

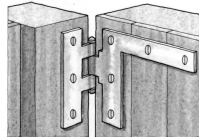

H-hinge

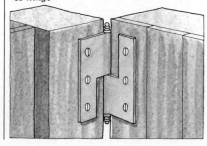

Ornamental T-hinge

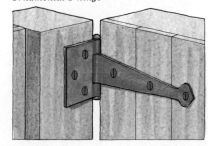

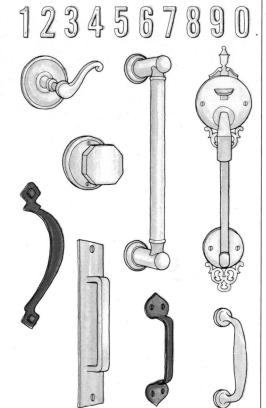

1234567890.

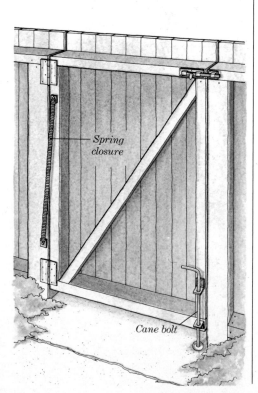

Spring closure

Cane bolt

BUILDING AND HANGING THE GATE

Select each piece of gate lumber carefully; it should be absolutely straight and true. Clear, kiln-dried, surfaced lumber is recommended, since it ensures the chances of the gate remaining flat and in square despite its exposure to the elements.

The basic construction process illustrated here is simple and straightforward and can be applied to the building of any gate, whether for a perimeter frame, as shown below, or for a Z-frame gate. It presents the sequence of steps in the order in which they should be done, though your own custom design might require additional steps along the way.

1. Measure the opening. Measure the distance between the posts at two points, at the bottom of the opening, and at the top. The measurement for the overall width of the gate consists of this post-to-post measurement, minus the basic (and essential) frame-to-gate post clearance allowance (½ to ¾ inch), plus whatever clearances are required by the hardware you use.

2. Cut the frame parts to length. The cross-members overlay the uprights so that water can't readily enter the joint. Cut the cross-members to length, then cut the uprights to fit between them. If using a special joint detail, prepare the joints now.

3. Assemble the frame. Nail or bolt the frame parts together, making sure that they are properly positioned to each other. A bolted frame is tremendously strong. Nails are apt to work loose, but the assembly can be made stronger with a good application of waterproof glue. The aim is to make the frame flat and in-square. To check it for square, measure the diagonals—from the outside corners of the cross-members. If the diagonal measurements are even, the frame is in-square. Use this same measuring technique for a Z-frame to make sure the parts are properly positioned.

Lay the frame down on the bracing member, which is to go from the hinge-side bottom to the latch-side top, and mark your cut lines. When you cut it to size, "save the line"—cutting just to the outside of your marks—so that the brace will have a tight fit. Then toenail the brace to the frame.

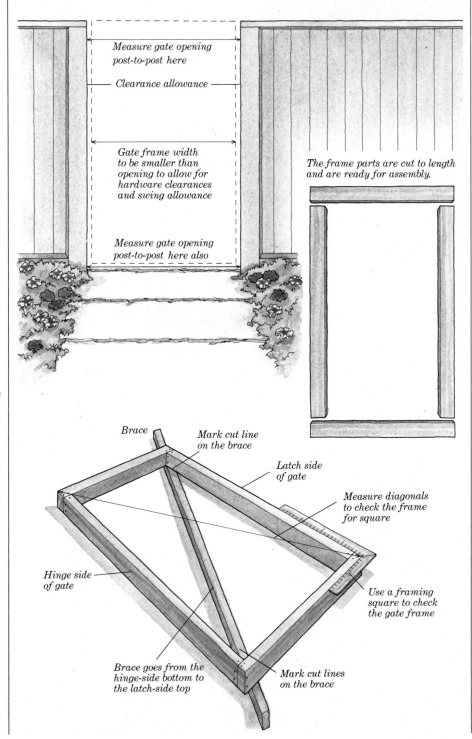

Measure gate opening post-to-post here

Clearance allowance

Gate frame width to be smaller than opening to allow for hardware clearances and swing allowance

Measure gate opening post-to-post here also

The frame parts are cut to length and are ready for assembly.

Brace

Mark cut line on the brace

Latch side of gate

Measure diagonals to check the frame for square

Hinge side of gate

Use a framing square to check the gate frame

Brace goes from the hinge-side bottom to the latch-side top

Mark cut lines on the brace

4. Add the infill. Put the frame down so that the surface to take the infill is facing you. *Is the brace going from the hinge-side bottom to the latch-side top? Make certain it is.* Then fasten down the infill and check it for proper alignment as you go. Use the same nailing techniques and guidelines described on pages 72-73 for fences.

5. Mount the hinges on the gate. Measure and mark the hinge positions. Drill pilot holes (make them slightly smaller than the shank of the screw) and fasten the gate leaf of the hinge to the gate. If you're using a wood stop, add it to the post now.

6. Check the fit. Gates, being heavy and a little awkward to handle, are easier to fit with the aid of a helper. Hold the gate in position and see if it will open and close without binding against the post. If necessary, trim the gate to give it clearance.

7. Hang the gate. Prop the fitted gate up in the opening and mark the hinge screw-hole positions on the post. Drill pilot holes and hang the gate. Measure and mark out the latch and catch positions, and mount the hardware on the gate and post. Finish the gate according to your finish treatment plan (see pages 57 and 61 for information about finishes).

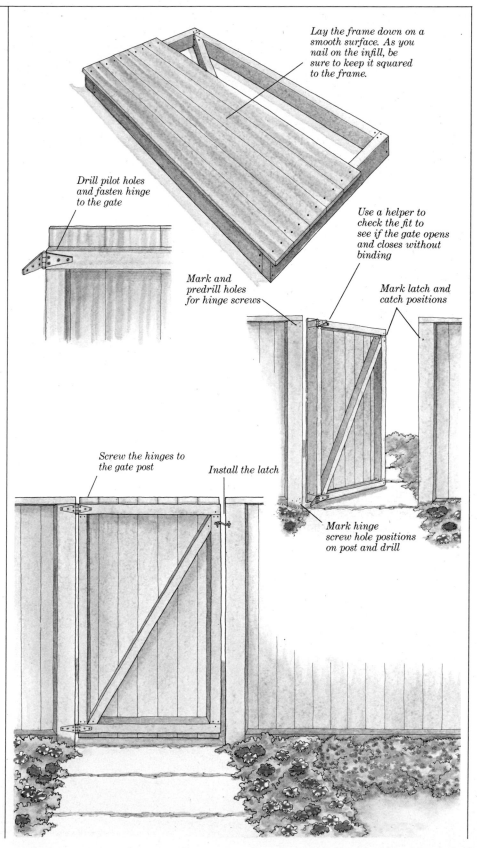

Lay the frame down on a smooth surface. As you nail on the infill, be sure to keep it squared to the frame.

Drill pilot holes and fasten hinge to the gate

Use a helper to check the fit to see if the gate opens and closes without binding

Mark and predrill holes for hinge screws

Mark latch and catch positions

Screw the hinges to the gate post

Install the latch

Mark hinge screw hole positions on post and drill

Technical Consultants

Many people contributed to the technical information included in this book. This list represents those contributors. Thanks to all.

Acorn Manufacturing Co., Inc.
Mansfield, MA

Action Fence
Concord, CA

Advanced Affiliates
Corona, NY

American Colorado Fence Co.
Denver, CO

American Plywood Association
Tacoma, WA

American Wood Preservers Institute
Vienna, VA

Arrowsmith Industries
Los Angeles, CA

Baldwin Hardware Mfg. Corp.
Reading, PA

Belwith International, Ltd.
City of Industry, CA

Creative Advertising Corp.
Warwick, RI

D-Mar Lumber & Hardware
Gardena, CA

Dale Lumber Company
Washington, DC

Fence Parts, Inc.
Fort Worth, TX

Furman Lumber Co.
Boston, MA

Gilbert & Bennett Mfg. Co.
Georgetown, CT

Hager Hardware
St. Louis, MO

Hollaender Mfg. Corp.
Cincinnati, OH

Hyde Park Products Corp.
New Rochelle, NY

Ideal Security Hardware
St. Paul, MN

IMPEX Associates, Ltd., Inc.
Englewood, NJ

Keystone Steel & Wire
Peoria, IL

The Langdale Co.
Valdosta, GA

Leslie-Locke
Lodi, OH

Lewis Hyman, Inc.
Hawthorne, CA

Liberty Hardware Mfg. Corp.
White Plains, NY

Luxury Landscape
Concord, CA

Montvale Fence Co.
Boston, MA

National Manufacturing Co.
Sterling, IL

Chuck Osborne Fences
Glendale, CA

Osmose
Buffalo, NY

Ornamental Iron Supply Depot
San Jose, CA

Diane Parker & Associates
Huntington, NY

Quality Wholesale Fence Co.
Cincinnati, OH

Quincey Mfg. Co., Inc.
Brooklyn, NY

Shannon Lumber Co.
Chicago, IL

Sheffield Plastics, Inc.
Sheffield, MA

Simpson Hardware
Los Angeles, CA

Southeastern Lumber
    Manufacturers Association
Forest Park, GA

Stanley Hardware
New Britain, CT

Superior Aluminum Products, Inc.
Russia, OH

Sutherland Lumber
Dallas, TX

Taco Products
Plainville, CT

Tennessee Fabricating Co.
Memphis, TN

Trans-Atlantic Co.
Philadelphia, PA

Triangle Brass Mfg. Co., Inc.
Los Angeles, CA

Tuff-Glass
Sacramento, CA

The Union Fork & Hoe Co.
Columbus, OH

Urfic, Inc.
Salem, OH

Valli & Colombo, Inc.
Duarte, CA

Warp Bros.
Chicago, IL

Western Red Cedar
    Lumber Association
Portland, OR

G.E. Wright Steel and Wire Co.
Worcester, MA

Index

A

Adding to fences, 74-75
Alternating-bay fences, 30

B

Bamboo fences, 38
Basket weave fences, 35
Batter boards, 62
Bays, 42
  dividing fence line into, 52, 54-55
Bleaches, 57
Board fences, 28-30, 50
Boundary fences, 6-7, 8-9
Boundary of property, 22, 62
Building codes, 22
Building the fence
  additions, 75
  cutting posts, 68
  digging postholes, 65
  hanging gates, 92-93
  installing stringers, 68-73
  marking postholes, 64-65
  mortised and dadoed joints, 67
  preinstallation prep work, 61
  setting posts, 66-67
  staking the layout, 62, 63
Building plans, 54-55
Buying materials, 58-59, 60, 90
  See also specific fence styles
  for fence additions, 74
  for footings, 60
  gate lumber, 92
  hardware, 90
  lumber, 58-59, 60, 92
  nails, 59
  plywood, 35, 59
  storage and handling, 61

C

Chain link fences, 40
Choosing a fence. See Design;
  Fence styles; Function
Clapboard fences, 36
Climate, lumber choice and, 58
Climate buffers, 17
Climbing plants, 25, 49
  fence deterioration from, 76
Concrete post footings, 53, 60
  repairing, 76-77
  setting posts in, 56, 67
Contracting, 56
Costs, 56, 58, 60
Custom designs, 26, 44-49
  hardware, 90

D

Design, 6-7, 12-13, 18-19, 24-25
  See also Fence styles
  choice of lumber and, 58

custom, 26, 44-49, 90
fence and post tops, 48-49
finishes, 57
gates, 80-89, 90-91
structural variations, 44-49
Digging postholes, 64
Double post-and-rail fences, 27
Drainbed, 42, 53, 65, 67
Duplex nail, 59

E

Earth-and-gravel footings, 53
  checking for rot, 76
  planning guidelines, 60
  setting posts in, 56, 67
Estimating costs, 60
Existing fence additions, 74-75

F

Featherboard fences, 29
Fence styles, 8-19, 24-41
  See also Design
  basket weave, 35
  board, 28-30, 50
  chain link, 40
  clapboard, 36
  double post-and-rail, 27, 50
  gates, 80-89
  glass, 39
  joints, 44
  lath, 32
  lattice, 34
  louver, 34
  mounting methods, 70-73
  ornamental iron, 41
  paling or stockade, 33, 50
  picket, 31, 50
  plastic and fiberglass, 39
  plywood, 35, 50, 88
  post-and-board, 27
  post-and-rail, 27, 50
  shingle, 37, 89
  slat, 31, 32, 50
  for slopes, 50
  stacked rail, 26
  stake, 33
  structural components, 42, 43
  tongue-and-groove, 36
  variations, 44-49
  wire mesh, 40
  wire-bound, 37, 38, 50
  wood materials, 44
Fence tops, 48-49
Fiberglass fences, 39
Filler, 42, 56, 67
Finish
  applying, 71
  for fence additions, 74
  maintaining, 76
  planning for, 56, 57

preinstallation application, 61
wood preservatives, 58
Footings, 42, 43, 52, 53, 64, 67
  buying materials for, 60
  checking for rot, 76
  drainbed, 42, 53, 65, 67
  filler, 42, 56, 67
  frost heave and, 53
  for gate posts, 53
  planning guidelines, 60
  postholes, 52, 64
  setting posts in, 67
Framework, 42, 43
  for gates, 86, 87
  post sizes and spacing, 52
  on slopes, 50, 51
  variations, 44-47
Frost heave, 53
Function, 7, 8-19, 21, 23
  of gates, 79-83

G

Gate posts, 53, 75, 84
Gates, 78-93
  clearances, 90
  designing, 22, 23, 80-89
  framework, 86-87, 92
  hardware, 84, 90-91, 93
  installing, 92-93
  planning, 22, 23, 52, 86
  stops, 86-87
  width of, 23, 85
Gate stops, 86-87
Glass fences, 39
Grape stake fences, 70
Gravel, 42, 53, 65, 67
  See also Earth-and-gravel footings

H

Hanging gates, 93
Hardware, 59, 84
Heartwood, 58
Hinges, 90, 93

I

Infill, 42, 43
  for gates, 86, 93
  inset, 71, 86
  installing, 56, 70-73
  materials and styles, 26-41
  nail-on, 70-71, 86
  sloping, 50

J

Joints, 44, 66, 67
  for gates, 86

L

Lap-joint grid fences, 30
Latches and catches, 90-91

Lath fences, 32
Lattice fences, 12-13, 34, 50
Lattice gate infill, 86
Layout, 54-55
  for additions, 74, 75
  for gates, 86-87
  staking, 56, 62, 63, 75
Legal considerations, 22, 62
Line posts, 53, 54, 55
  setting, 66-67
Location of fence, 20-23
Louver fences, 34
Lumber
  See also specific types
  buying, 58-60
  dimensions, 60
  estimating cost of, 60
  preinstallation work, 61
  storage and handling, 61

M

Mending fences, 76-77
Metal fences, 26, 40, 41
Metal gates, 81, 82, 89
Mullion, 75

N

Nailing stringers, 68-71
Nail-on infill, 70-71, 86
Nails, 59
Noise buffers, 16-17

O

Obstructions, 50-51
Ornamental iron fences, 41
Ornamental iron gates, 81, 82

P

Paints, 56, 57
Paling (stockade) fences, 33, 50
Perimeter-frame gates, 86, 92-93
Picket fences, 8-9, 18-19, 25, 31
  cutting to length, 70
  for slopes, 50
Planning, 20-23, 42-55, 56
  additions to fences, 74
  choosing materials, 58-59
  gate openings, 22, 23, 52
  gates, 84-87, 90-91
  preparing to build, 56-61
Plantings, 25, 49
  deterioration from, 76
Plastic fences, 39
Plastic gate infill, 86
Plywood fences, 35, 88
  buying plywood, 35, 59
  with stepped framework, 50
Plywood gate infill, 86
Pole fences, 26
Post-and-board fences, 27
Post-and-rail fences, 27, 50

Postholes, 42, 52, 60
  digging, 56, 64-65
Posts, 42
  cutting, 68
  mortised or dadoed, 67
  repairing, 76-77
  setting, 56, 66-67
  sizes, 52, 60
  spacing, 22, 52, 54-55, 64, 65
  trees as, 51
  variations, 48-49
Pressure-treated lumber, 58
Primers, 57, 61
Privacy fences, 10-11
Property lines, 22, 62

R
Rail fences, 25, 26, 27
Rail gates, 78-79

Reed fences, 38
Repairing fences, 76-77
Rot resistance
  drainbed, 42, 53, 65, 67
  lumber choice and, 58

S
Screws, 90
Sealers, 57, 61
Security fencing, 14-15
Setting posts, 60, 66-67
Shingle fences, 37
  gate for, 89
Site plan, 20-23
Slat fences, 10-11, 32, 50
Slopes, 50-51
  gate design for, 85
  marking postholes on, 64
Snow fencing, 37
Stacked-rail fences, 26

Stains, 57
Stake fences, 33, 50
Staking the layout, 56, 62, 63
  for additions, 75
Stepped framework, 50, 51
Stockade fences, 33, 50
Stringers, 42
  installing, 44-47, 56, 68-73
  on slopes, 50-51
Structural considerations
  fence styles and, 24-41
  footings, 53
  gates, 84-87
  joints, 44
  plywood and, 59
  repair, 76-77
  slopes and obstructions, 50-51
  stringer positions, 45-47

T
Terminal posts, 53, 54, 55
  posthole depth, 60
  setting, 66
Tongue-and-groove fences, 36
Trees, mounting infill on, 51
Turnbuckle gate supports, 85

W
Wire mesh fences, 40
Wire-and-wheel gate supports, 85
Wire-bound fences, 37, 38, 50
Wood preservatives, 58

Z
Z-frame gates, 86, 87, 92

U.S. Measure and Metric Measure Conversion Chart

		Formulas for Exact Measures			Rounded Measures for Quick Reference		
	Symbol	When you know:	Multiply by	To find:			
Mass (Weight)	oz	ounces	28.35	grams	1 oz		= 30 g
	lb	pounds	0.45	kilograms	4 oz		= 115 g
	g	grams	0.035	ounces	8 oz		= 225 g
	kg	kilograms	2.2	pounds	16 oz	= 1 lb	= 450 kg
					32 oz	= 2 lb	= 900 kg
					36 oz	= 2 1/4 lb	= 1000g (a kg)
Volume	tsp	teaspoons	5.0	milliliters	1/4 tsp	= 1/24 oz	= 1 ml
	tbsp	tablespoons	15.0	milliliters	1/2 tsp	= 1/12 oz	= 2 ml
	fl oz	fluid ounces	29.57	milliliters	1 tsp	= 1/6 oz	= 5 ml
	c	cups	0.24	liters	1 tbsp	= 1/2 oz	= 15 ml
	pt	pints	0.47	liters	1 c	= 8 oz	= 250 ml
	qt	quarts	0.95	liters	2 c (1 pt)	= 16 oz	= 500 ml
	gal	gallons	3.785	liters	4 c (1 qt)	= 32 oz	= 1 l
	ml	milliters	0.034	fluid ounces	4 qt (1 gal)	= 128 oz	= 3 3/4-l
Length	in.	inches	2.54	centimeters	3/8 in.		= 1 cm
	ft	feet	30.48	centimeters	1 in.		= 2.5 cm
	yd	yards	0.9144	meters	2 in.		= 5 cm
	mi	miles	1.609	kilometers	2-1/2 in.		= 6.5 cm
	km	kilometers	0.621	miles	12 in. (1 ft)		= 30 cm
	m	meters	1.094	yards	1 yd		= 90 cm
	cm	centimeters	0.39	inches	100 ft		= 30 m
					1 mi		= 1.6 km
Temperature	°F	Fahrenheit	5/9 (after subtracting 32)	Celsius	32°F		= 0°C
					68°F		= 20°C
	°C	Celsius	9/5 (then add 32)	Fahrenheit	212°F		= 100°C
Area	in.²	square inches	6.452	square centimeters	1 in.²		= 6.5 cm²
	ft²	square feet	929.0	square centimeters	1 ft²		= 930 cm²
	yd²	square yards	8361.0	square centimeters	1 yd²		= 8360 cm²
	a	acres	0.4047	hectares	1 a		= 4050 m²